MORE THAN A MEMORY

REFLECTIONS OF VIET NAM

ED. BY VICTOR R. VOLKMAN

Reflections of History Series
Modern History Press

More than a Memory: Reflections of Viet Nam
Book #5 in the Reflections of History Series
Copyright © 2009 Victor R. Volkman. All Rights Reserved.
All contributors retain rights to their original works.

Cover photo used with permission from TheCombatReport.com.
"My Blue Block of Wood" by Richard Boes, PFC excerpted with permission from *The Last Dead Soldier Alive*.
"Expended Casings" and other poems by Alan Farrell excerpted with permission from *Expended Casings*.
"Present Day" by Don Bodey used with permission from *F.N.G, 2nd Ed.*.
"Torque in Angkor Wat" by Marc Levy originally published on slow-trains.com (2005).
"How Stevie Nearly Lost the War" by Marc Levy. Originally published in *New Millennium Writings*, Issue 14 (2004-2005). Reproduced with permission.
"Whatever You Did in War Will Always Be With You" by Marc Levy excerpted with permission from *CounterPunch* Vol. 13. No. 11, June 2006.
"America's Black Monument" by Richard Levine was originally published in *Medicinal Purposes Literary Review*. Reproduced with permission.
"Mud-Walking" by Richard Levine originally appeared in Rattapallax #3.

Library of Congress Cataloging-in-Publication Data
More than a memory : reflections of Viet Nam / ed. by Victor R. Volkman.
   p. cm. -- (Reflections of history series ; v. 5)
  Includes bibliographical references and index.
  ISBN-13: 978-1-932690-64-4 (trade paper : alk. paper)
  ISBN-10: 1-932690-64-6 (trade paper : alk. paper)
  ISBN-13: 978-1-932690-65-1 (hardcover : alk. paper)
  ISBN-10: 1-932690-65-4 (hardcover : alk. paper)
 1. Vietnam War, 1961-1975--Literary collections. 2. Veterans' writings, American. 3. Vietnam War, 1961-1975--Personal narratives, American. I. Volkman, Victor R.
  PS509.V53M67 2008
  810.8'0358--dc22
                                       2008018187

Modern History Press　　　　　http://ModernHistoryPress.com
an imprint of Loving Healing Press　info@ModernHistoryPress.com
5145 Pontiac Trail　　　　　　　　Tollfree 888-761-6268
Ann Arbor, MI 48105　　　　　　　Fax 734-663-6861
USA

Modern History Press

REFLECTIONS OF HISTORY SERIES

- My Tour in Hell: A Marine's Battle with Combat Trauma by David W. Powell
- Made in America, Sold in the Nam: A Continuing Legacy of Pain. Ed by Rick Ritter and Paul Richards
- Giving My Heart: Love in a Military Family by Lisa H. Farber-Silk
- F.N.G.: Revised Edition by Don Bodey
- More Than A Memory: Reflections of Viet Nam. Ed by Victor R. Volkman
- Iraq Through A Bullet Hole: A Civilian Returns Home by Issam Jameel

Contents

Acknowledgments	iii
About the Cover	iii
Foreword	v
Chapter 1 – Richard Boes: *My Blue Block of Wood*	7
Chapter 2 – Poetry	21
Alan Farrell: *Nothing So Bad It's Not Poetry*	21
Preston Hood: *Rung Sat*	24
Jim Murphy: *Scapular*	26
Martin H. Ray: *Saigon, 1972*	27
Dayl Wise: *The Cross of St. Andrew*	28
Chapter 3 – David W. Powell: *An Office in Hell*	31
Chapter 4 – Poetry	43
Alan Farrell: *Expended Casings*	43
Preston Hood: *Alive or Dead*	44
Dayl Wise: *Walking My Dog While at War*	45
Tony Swindell: *Suicide in the Jungle*	46
Richard Levine: *Memorial Day*	47
Richard Levine: *Home from War*	48
Marc Levy: *At Nineteen*	49
Chapter 5 – Don Bodey: *Present Day*	51
Chapter 6 – Poetry	65
Richard Levine: *America's Black Monument*	65
Preston Hood: *Purgatory*	67
Richard Levine: *Survivor Guilt*	68
Dayl Wise: *Pop Smoke*	69
Marc Levy: *Peace Time*	70
Dayl Wise: *Vietnam Revisited*	72
Chapter 7 – Tom Skiens: Witness to Rape	73
Chapter 8 – Poetry	79
Preston Hood: *Boats near Hue, Viet Nam, 1997*	79
Richard Levine: *Birnam Wood*	80
Dayl Wise: *The Woods Move*	81
Jim Murphy: *The Great Imprinting Event at Quang Tri*	83
Tony Swindell: *Call It Sleep*	86

Alan Farrell: *The Man Who Outlived His Lieutenant*   88
Richard Levine: *Mud-Walking*   92

Chapter 9 – Marc Levy: *How Stevie Nearly Lost the War*   93

Chapter 10 – Shirley Jolls and Walter Aponte: *Kangaroo Court Martial*   109

Chapter 11 – Poetry   121
Dayl Wise: *Found Photograph*   121
Alan Farrell: *Fighting Position*   123
Alan Farrell: *The Tom*   125

Chapter 12 – Rich Raitano: *Absent of Grace and Mercy*   133

Chapter 13 – Poetry   147
Preston Hood: *At the Wall*   147
Alan Farrell: *On Catching Sight of an M-188 Tracked Recovery Vehicle...*   149
Tom Skiens: *Rally Round the Flag, Boys*   151

Chapter 14 – Marc Levy: *Torque in Angkor Wat*   157

Chapter 15 – Pieter van Aggelen: *A South African in Viet Nam*   165

Chapter 16 – Martin H. Ray: *The Face of the Enemy*   175

Chapter 17 – David Bianchini: *Letter to Shane*   181

Chapter 18 – Tom Skiens: *Boat People*   187

Chapter 19 – Marc Levy: *Off the Road*   191

Chapter 20 – Marc Levy: *Whatever You Did in War Will Always be With You*   201

About The Contributors   205

Glossary   209

Index   219

Acknowledgments

This book was inspired by a conversation with social writing activist Anya Achtenberg who introduced me to Preston Hood, and subsequently a network of many thoughtful and articulate vet writers.

A book like this is not even remotely possible without the trust, encouragement, and full participation of the contributors. I will thank them all, in alphabetical order: David Bianchini, Don Bodey, Richard Boes, Alan Farrell, Preston Hood, Richard Levine, Marc Levy, Bob Moore, Jim Murphy, David W. Powell, Rich Raitano, Martin H. Ray, Tom Skeins, Tony Swindell, Pieter van Aggelen, and Dayl Wise. Kyle Morgan of *The Combat Report* researched photos for the cover.

A special thank you to Marc Levy for helping me to proofread the first draft and establish a professional style and uniform presentation for this sprawling work. Matthew Farrell proofread the second draft and his comments improved both grammatical and historical accuracy.

My work with Rick Ritter on *Made In America: Sold In The 'Nam, 2nd Ed.* (2006) was invaluable in giving me a better understanding of what a Viet Nam vet anthology could do. It is my humble hope that this book can follow the trail that Paul Richards' first edition of *Made in America: Sold in the 'Nam* blazed in 1985.

About the Cover

The cover photo depicts a machine gun crew of the III Marine Amphibious Force ("III MAF") defending Hill 170 during Operation Essex (Nov. 5-17, 1967). The A-Gunner insures the proper flow of the ammunition belt and his left hand rests on the replacement barrel for when the M-60 inevitably overheats. The helmet buttons read "We Try Harder!" Originally the motto of Avis Rent-A-Car, it was later adopted by various combat units. Photograph by Cpl G. E. Aker. Used with permission.

Foreword

> "The point of a story can penetrate far deeper than the point of any bullet."
> —Lawrence Nault, *The Mountain Hermit*

Why another Viet Nam book? That's a question that I've heard from more than one person. Isn't it over…aren't people so "done" with that? Four decades on, the pain is still there for those who served willingly or unwillingly. And it continues to echo onward in the lives of their children and spouses. In the words of disabled veteran, author, and social worker Rick Ritter: "War still sucks."

There are two lessons to be learned. First, that the essential nature of warfare remains unchanged. A quick browse through the poetry of WWI veteran Siegfried Sassoon)confirms that chaos, confusion, and carnage are constant. Sure, we have come a long way from backbreaking battlefield radios into cell phones and even live-video feeds, but the human experience of war is not less horrifying no matter how much technology you throw into a war.

Second, the idea that "time changes nothing" for those who have experienced armed conflict and casualties. Many can call up vivid multi-sensory recollections including taste, smells, and sights at a moment's notice, and these sense-perceptions can be triggered by things as innocuous and innocent as the time of the *year*.

And yet hope and healing is possible for men and women who have fought. I could not take the helm of such a project if I felt it was impossible. The soul can come to terms with experience and be richer for it. The telling of stories is therapeutic and is confirmed in exposure techniques such as Traumatic Incident Reduction (TIR), in which pure, unjudged, and uninterrupted storytelling produces catharsis and relief. For it is those stories that we don't understand, can't comprehend, refuse to accept which shackle the soul. On a larger scale, Truth and Reconciliation commissions in South Africa produced a level of healing merely by allowing everyone to acknowledge what had happened.

If you are a veteran, I hope you will take the opportunity to tell your story in a safe environment. I urge you to consider attending one of the Spiritual Healing Workshops put on by the International Conference of War Veteran Ministers (VietnamVeteranMinisters.org).

If you are a civilian, my wish is that you carry away some understanding of what can happen in the volatile world of the battlefield, and how that world leaves marks on the soul. Say *thank you* to a veteran. This volume is my way of doing the same.

Victor R. Volkman, Senior Editor
Modern History Press
November, 1st, 2008

1 My Blue Block of Wood
Richard Boes

> "He who learns must suffer
> And even in our sleep pain that cannot forget
> Falls drop by drop upon the heart,
> And in our own despite, against our will,
> Comes wisdom to us by the awful grace of God."
>
> From *Agamemnon* by Aeschlyus

It was a plane full of strangers, a hundred and fifty of us maybe, but no one I remembered or seemed to know from a year ago. Just this deafening silence like the kind that stops you at the moment somethin' or someone dies. Jesus, it ain't me anymore reflected in the window glass but ghosts, faces I'd known, Buttkins, Henderson, Walsh, Casey-fuckin'-Jones. A backdrop of flares, tracer bullets, an explosion here and there like fireworks across a black screen, a black sky, a black hole we were shooting out of as we taxied down the runway.

Even in this pressurized cabin, the heat still clung to my flesh, the stench, the taste of burnt, rotting corpses still permeated the air. You couldn't wash it off, there hadn't been time, no debriefing, besides it was stuck in my throat, suspended somehow between home and my gut.

We were all in jungle fatigues, worn and faded green, muddy, some ripped, others bloodstained. As was the practice, I'd crossed off days on a pocket calendar, sealed tight in a personalized, plastic, First Cav, waterproof wallet. Still, though the ink bled, eventually I called myself "Short!"

"Short! Three days and a wake-up," Brown yelped. Now this here was the fuckin' wake-up, I was in tow, goin' back to the world. Thinking, couldn't stop myself, all the things I'd truly missed, all the things I'd do. Still, I sat in disbelief. *Why me?*

I couldn't stop my legs from moving, up and down, side to side, in and out of time. There was a chorus stirring about me, a rustling movement goin' nowhere. That final fear resonated in everyone's eyes, what if we take a fucking rocket? What if we crash? After all this shit, the irony, Jesus, wouldn't it be my luck? I continued my search back and forth, front to back as if scanning a perimeter, a fuckin' treeline. It wasn't the enemy I was looking for, not this time, but someone, anyone

I might recognize. No one, it seemed. We'd all been abandoned by a meaningless war, forsaken on all fronts, both sides, both for and against. Even to ourselves we were strangers. God was absent. I was alone.

A tour of duty was a year, troops coming and going every day like a shift-change entering or leaving a factory. Dispersed, replaced, gathered up, and sent off. This was very much an individual war. I'd left everyone in my platoon, my company, behind as others had previously left me. I wasn't supposed to care. I didn't! When Myles left a few months earlier, he cried and held me in his arms. He was drunk. O'Brien borrowed ten bucks he was gonna mail to me, but six days back in the world he deliberately drove off a bridge in his brand-new red Corvette. And Casey, Casey re-upped for the fuckin' dope. This war was about getting me out alive, and up to now I'd been victorious.

The pilot broke the silence announcing over the PA, "Gentlemen, we've just cleared Viet Nam airspace." We all cheered, but it was like someone trying to laugh who can't stop crying, like trying to make small talk at your best friend's funeral. Quickly, the silence returned. I couldn't stop my legs from pumping. There in the glass were only shadows of who I once was, who I didn't recognize anymore, a fuckin' ghost.

I do, I do believe… I do. Smacking my knees together, these muddy boots like ruby red slippers. It's over. I'm going. *I'm goin' home.*

We stopped twice briefly to refuel, once in Thailand, then Hawaii, and eighteen hours later landed in California. We were bused to a military base. No wire mesh on the windows anymore to repel explosive cocktails, no fires in the skies like when I got to the war. No heat, no stench clinging to my flesh, but this one, this taste I'd brought home in my mouth like the promise of milk and honey gone sour. There wasn't any fanfare, there was no one. We walked through a barn door, the back door of a building, a basement entrance, down a long corridor of bare bulbs and concrete, what looked like a warehouse, a slaughterhouse, or even a fuckin' prison… like I was gonna be interrogated, tortured, or somethin', somethin' bad. And over the archway was a sign that read, "Your Country's Proud of You."

"Fuck you!" shouted someone. Others laughed, or tried to.

"The joke's on us," I told the guy to my right, who tossed up a middle finger. Some officer in clean-starched khakis, donning a blonde, butch, stuck-up haircut, broke us down in columns and pointed us in which directions to go.

"Welcome home, welcome home, welcome home," he whispered as we passed in rows of two. No one saluted, and I could tell we made him nervous.

Welcome home motherfucker! was my only thought, as I pretended to trip and bumped him up against a wall. "Excuse me, Sir."

I took a shower, a fuckin' hot shower, and got me a change of clothes. Goddamn dress greens! I wasn't thrilled about having to wear a uniform. Besides the stories of being spit upon and the name-calling, a rumor was circulating that a woman approached a soldier in a commercial airport, identified the patch on his arm as being the same as her son's, same as mine, he'd been killed. She wailed, "Why are you still alive?" pulled a gun from her purse and shot him dead.

Some spiffy soldier, a fuckin' paper-shuffler, sat behind a desk and asked if we had any wounds he needed to make note of. "Speak now, or forget about it." His name tag read "Pilot," all the hair he'd left on his head like cotton balls was in his ears. God was here, alive, and laughing.

"I'm fine," I told him, ignoring the shrapnel that was still in my leg. "I just wanna go home." There was a free steak dinner, but no one I knew of was hungry for food. I collected my things, and soon enough was on a plane back East, and homeward bound.

It was sometime after midnight and the airport was practically empty. In a day's time, I'd traveled from the hellish jungles of war and was just a forty-five minute car ride from home. I'd called Jimmy, my best friend since childhood, and he was en route. My family expected me sometime during the month, but had no idea I was soon to arrive. It felt strange wearing dress greens and not jungle fatigues, bright ribbons and patches instead of camouflage. These new shoes only hurt my feet, I missed my muddy boots. Still, I couldn't sit still and wait, but had to walk around.

All the shops were closed. I was too young for the bar, too young to vote, too young for anything, but not to die. So few people around, and those who did pass avoided eye contact. I wanted so badly to celebrate, to yell out as fucking loud as I could, I'm home! To grab some girl and dance, dance the fuckin' skies like an angel, to sweep her off her feet with a passionate kiss. Like that photograph, that other war, a war that meant somethin', but no one seemed to notice me, no one cared. I was fuckin' invisible. I didn't fit. I didn't belong here. I might even welcome someone calling me a bad name, at least to show I'm alive. Me, the keeper of a lost war, a war no one seemed to recognize, or desired any knowledge of. Jesus, it's all that I'm about anymore. And if I could I'd fuckin' disappear like you wish I would. *If!* If only I could. And the enemy was silent, and the silence was killing me.

I tried saying something to someone, anyone, say anything like, what time is it? Nice weather we're having. Have you change for a dollar? Excuse me, Miss, my name is Lazarus, I'm back from the dead, and I ain't got a fuckin' clue.

This underwear I hadn't worn for a year, buttoned-up collar and tie, irritated the jungle rot, the pimpled sores that oozed in a straight line from the base of my neck to the balls of my crotch. There's too much starch in this shirt. I itched like a fuckin' leper on parade, a bad case of mistaken identity, and, and I had to pee. Where's the men's room? I could ask, but fuck it. I'd find it myself.

I lost the tie and unbuttoned a few buttons down my shirt, took the bayonet strapped to my leg and cut my underwear off. The bathroom was empty, so I thought, standing at the urinal having a good scratch, taking a leak, caught unawares as the janitor came out from the toilet area and dropped a large trash drum to the floor. *Incoming!*

Shrapnel flies up and out, hot and screaming, so the lower you get the better your chances. In a split-second's nosedive, I was flat against the earth sucking up warm wet tile in a puddle of my own piss. A moment's flash and I'm back there, had I ever left? Where the fuck am I now?

"Sorry boy, you's okay?" A soft, black, gray-whiskered face was leaning over me.

"Yeah," I said, "guess so," feeling only grateful it wasn't a rocket. He handed me a towel from around his neck.

"Dry's yourself," he winked a surprising sky-blue glass eye, scratched with fat nervous fingers atop his thinning hair. "*Sold*, it's the first four letters of soldier, a four-letter word," he laughed, a disheartened-like punch-drunk fighter's wheeze. "And your sellin' price," shooin' a fly from his face, "wasn't even our freedom. My name's Elijah," he took up his mop. "There's no good wars to speak about, but at least my's generation, our war had a purpose."

"Thanks," I said as he took back his towel, and shook my hand.

"Wars is fought by us poor folk, us soldiers, is niggers, and all niggers is trained to die." He itched with a flurry of pokes at his nose. "Don't you let them make it your fault. You's hear me boy?" I just nodded my head and made my way for the exit. Elijah fumbled twice, dropped his mop to the floor. I wanted to catch it, but was too far off, too slow, too late. He called out as the door closed between us. "You's be a survivor."

Me and Jimmy were both more than tired. He was against the war, an accountant now, not much for words. I didn't know what to say, or how to say it. We talked sports some, the Mets had won the World Series, the Jets the Super Bowl, the Knicks were NBA champs. Other than him reading every street sign, billboard, storefront we passed, we were mostly quiet. "Shop Rite," "Two Guys", "Kool, come up, all the way up." Yeah, I was feeling anxious, afraid, guilty I think about coming home.

Elijah was right. It wasn't my fault, it wasn't up to me. I didn't choose to be there, who would die, and who would come back. And there ain't no more Stockwell, Abrams, Smyth, or Donny Gains. Jesus, and Rodney Brown who stood where I stood just moments before. "Short! Three days and a wake-up," he yelped in a black man's drawl. "I's goin' back to the world! I's one lucky motherfucker!" and Betty, Bouncin' Betty, she's a goddamn landmine, bounced up in his lap, cut 'im in fuckin' two! And a B-40 rocket swallowed what was left into tiny little fucking pieces.

"Don't mean nothin'!" Myles said.

And I'll never know by just how much I missed her. Half a step maybe, *If!* Guess I'm one, one lucky motherfucker! Just these shards, bits of metal in my leg. And one, Rodney's one patch of black hair sunken in behind one eye swimming in a sea of brain matter, all pink, and blue, and gray. We collected him in a black bag, "I'm in pieces, bits and pieces!" Me and Myles kept singing, stomped our feet, scattered the fucking bits that weren't even pieces anymore.

You're really alone during a rocket attack, there's nothin' anyone can do. You're really fuckin' alone, when the other guy's dead. *If!* As if he'd taken my place. And if you're one of the lucky ones you get to do it again. And again. And the repetition, over, over, and again. And the pieces that won't fit together like Humpty Dumpty didn't have to pick himself up. And all the King's horses wear blinders, and all the King's men believe their own lies. "Don't mean nothin'!" And the fucking fear that resonates, echoes back and forth, gnaws and eats away at you, over, over, and again. It's worse than death. I do believe, I don't believe you. And who's the lucky motherfucker?

We sat at the tracks waiting for the train to pass. Its whistle and pulsing bark put me on edge, my feet on fuckin' trampolines. Here I was alone again, with Jimmy in the driver's seat, still waiting. I tried counting cars, seven, seventeen, seventy-eight, how many more before I'm home safe? The face in the windshield was Rodney's. All I really wanted was to be held, for someone to hold me.

Me and Jimmy met some twelve years ago, he was a few years older and my family'd just moved into the neighborhood. I had this old beat-up glove that was my Dad's and a blue block of wood I was using for a ball. I was throwing it high up against the side brick of the house and making basket catches like Willie Mays. The whole game was alive in my head, both teams, a miss was a run and it was one-one, in the bottom of the sixteenth. Jimmy approached unnoticed until he sneezed, a giant fuckin' sneeze. He was a tall skinny kid with a face like Goofy, a dried mop of brown hair, and a big long tweaked nose. I'd made a bad throw, and just missed catching it with a diving attempt into the bushes. "Nice try," he said, and goofed up a laugh like a jackass hee-haws. "That's it, game's over, you lose!" Jimmy invited me to join him and his friends up the block, the Dick Street Bombers. They had a real ball, and needed a center fielder.

In a few weeks I was to be the best man at Jimmy's wedding.

Sure we were happy to see each other, but something was missing, it just wasn't the same. Yeah, guess it was me who'd changed. I wanted to tell him about the war, about Rodney, what I'd seen and done, but didn't know how, couldn't find the words. Anyway, I didn't think he'd understand.

We were just a few miles from home and I had to say somethin', flush this spin-cycle circlin' my brain, break my fuckin' silence. I mentioned meeting Elijah, him helping me up off the floor, and the conversation that followed. Suddenly and without warning, Jimmy's Mustang jumped the curb. He'd fallen asleep on me, and we were headed straight on for a telephone pole. The second thu-thump of the back tires woke him the fuck up. "Jesus!" he shrieked, but was slow to react. In one sweeping motion I reached over and cut the wheel to the left landing us back on the street. Jim was a bit shaken up, squeezed tight. "Sorry," he said, "coulda killed us."

"Don't mean nothin'!" I told 'im, and for a moment I was baggin' Rodney again. "Just stay awake, Jim. We're almost home." I never called him Jim. Something felt good inside, this wasn't like a rocket attack, there was more I could do than just be a passenger.

"See ya man, thanks for the ride." I closed the car door, Jimmy drove off. The house was all dark, no porch light left burning. Bones, my dog must of come home, but there ain't no barkin'. I climbed the steps, hit all the fuckin' cracks down the walk, another flight of steps. They never locked the front door, but something stopped me from opening it. I turned myself around, gazing up at the streetlight. A pair of my old sneakers still hung by their laces over telephone wire, deep blue shadow sifted through naked tree branches like distant fingers, reaching into, grabbing at a big thick slice of pitch-black, heavenly mud-pie. No stars. Still no Bones.

Mom, Dad, my two younger brothers and sisters were inside sleeping. I felt this knot in my stomach like the whole fucking war was twisting up inside me, might I just fuckin' implode! I wouldn't wake them, I'd go quietly upstairs and go to bed. I'd see them come mornin'. I opened the screen door, stopped, and had to close it, opened and closed it again. Walked round the side of the house, doubled over, body doubled up, holdin' my stomach, leaned into some bushes and started throwing up. Once, twice, over and again until there was nothin', nothin' but bile, yellow sauce, until all of me was empty, inside and out. And there, right the fuck before my eyes, peering out at me, out from under dead leaves and a fresh spray of vomit was my blue block of wood. I scooped it up as if I'd found lost treasure, gold and silver bullion, and cleaned it off with a few swipes against the grass. I clenched it in my fist, couldn't help but smile. Bones came running up, his blackness all a-glow, excited and welcoming me home.

I looked in for a moment at my youngest brother Billy, my godchild sleeping peacefully. As a child I was a sound sleeper, I once fell off the top bunk of a bunk bed and didn't wake up. Hearing the thud, my parents came rushing in from the living room and found me sleeping on the floor Now I had to put my mattress on the floor, and it was a good thing that my room was the smallest in the house, most like a bunker, less of a target, it provided a false sense of security. Accustomed as I was to the constant barrage of noise a war makes, now the silent night of suburbia was keeping me awake.

AFter only a few weeks in Viet Nam I knew every sound of darkness like a blind man knows his own home. What was incoming and cause for alarm, and what was going out. I slept on a thin dime, and the faint whistle of a distant rocket would call me out from a crowded dream. I'd be hugging mother earth like a babe for milk, sucking up mud like wanting breath, steel pot and flak jacket on. I'd have a fuckin' cigarette lit before the first round hit, before any siren ever sounded. *If!* And if it let up long enough you ran for a bunker.

I came to know with acute precision, like a fine-tuned instrument, the difference, the distinction in every sound the blackness made. What were rockets, mortars, short rounds, a.k.a. friendly fire, *snafu*! Fred took one in the shower. Small-arms, M-60s, M-79s, quad-50s, B-52s, and oh how the ground shook. Flares, Claymores, bounce, fuckin' Bouncin' Betty, fuck! Fuckin' B-40! *If!* A sapper left a satchel charge in a hooch two doors down. Don't mean nothin'! A luring Loach, whoop, whoop, whoop, draws out enemy fire, a seething Cobra and other gunships closin' in. Woof! Napalm jet streamers, and Puff, Puff the Magic Dragon, whose mini-guns from on high could infiltrate every fuckin' square inch of space the size of a football field in a matter of seconds. Every twenty-seventh round was a tracer, and we watched cheering atop a bunker as the red whip, the red whip waved on, and on, and fuckin' on like hells bells rainin' down.

We were the supreme, ultimate firepower of the skies. Absolute, all-powerful, like God I thought, like God lacks humility. But the enemy was underground, tunneled in beneath the earth, at the core of believing, beyond extinction.

Now I scanned about my room by the gray-blue shadows of moon, and filtering streetlight, beads like tears patterned upon embroidered curtain lace. In the wake of the battle, tired enough, but unable to sleep. The rug was sky blue and grape-juice stained, the walls needed more than paint. Jesus was missing limbs on the crucifix above, at the back of my brain, broken off by a touchdown pass that should have been caught. Dust collectors on bookshelves posing as trophies, old posters, banners, signed baseballs and other sports memorabilia. My bruised blue block of wood I'd placed on the dresser, my bayonet sheathed, asleep under my pillow. That picture, without any glass, a gentle boy laid back on a hillside, all blue-jeans, white button-down shirt, red-vested, black shiny curls, an arm up shielding his eyes from the sun. Tell me, tell me again... please, tell me your dreams?

Football is the precursor to war, the training fields, the same language. Kill, kill, kill! War is the ultimate sport, the culmination of sport. Kill, or be killed! Kill the Giants, Jets, Patriots, and Eagles. Kill the fuckin' Yankees, Braves, and Angels. Kill Babe Ruth! Killroy, he's not here anymore. Kill Jim Brown, John Brown, Charlie Brown, and Rodney Brown. "I's one lucky motherfucker!" Kill the fuckin' Gooks! Kill the Japs, the Krauts, the Commies, and the Jews. Kill Goliath! John the Baptist, John the Catholic, his brother Bobby, and Martin Luther King Jr.!

"My God, My God, why hast Thou forsaken me?" Kill Jesus! And like Cain slew Abel, I am the plowman, the keeper of a bad uprooted seedling, maimed and forced to wander. And Abraham, what of Isaac? Kill me!

Bones rests his head on my belly, looks up at me, gives me a stare like what the fuck man, like he knows my thoughts like he feels bad for me because I'm a fuckin' nut job! "Good old Bones."

It's raining now, a soothing rain, rap, a pat, tap, and the occasional swish of a passing motorist endeavoring to lull me to sleep. It's not that hard monsoon rain that blinds the sky, or the sound of hot screaming metal cavorting off tin roofs, that piercing screech that howls and rips through tent canvas embedding itself below the heart at gut-level.

Uncle Ho's birthday, I couldn't stop the thoughts. We were hit five times during the night with over ninety rockets. Every time I'd fall asleep. Again, over and over. We got no fuckin' sleep. From side to side, closer, overhead, then passing. Back and forth like walking giants. Giant steps. Explosive, deafening! Fe, fi, fo, fum! *If!* If one hits the roof you're dead! Away, and back again. Approaching, closer, fi, fo, fum! *If!* If one hits the roof, and again! Over and again like the buttoning and unbuttoning of shirts until all the buttons fall off.

I'd promised God I'd go to church every Sunday for the rest of my life. *If!* If he'd just get me the fuck outta here alive. The hooch in front of us was hit, and all twelve guys obliterated. The tent to the right, the one behind were all gone now. And still came the giants. Fi, fo, fum! And Casey, Casey took one in the shithouse while shootin' up at the war. Happy fuckin' trails! Swishhhhhh.

My eyes pop open, toothpick wide! This ain't no fuckin' war, this is my room, there's Bones asleep on the floor like old paint. Please, dear God, but for thy grace, grant us some fuckin' sleep. Rap, a-pat, tap. Fe, fi, fo, there are no giants anymore. Swishhhhhh.

We sat on empty ammo boxes under a sweltering sky in twelve rows of five. It was Palm Sunday, my first Sunday in Viet Nam and the last time I attended Mass. A Major, a priest who resembled Elijah, stood before us in bloody, torn jungle fatigues and addressed us as a group. The blood was blue. "I haven't time to hear your confessions, so just think of your sins, and you's forgiven." He made the sign of the cross pendulating his rifle muzzle through the air. I hadn't sinned yet, my uniform was clean. I was nothin', an FNG, a fuckin' new guy. What the fuck did I know? Was this ammo box really empty?

The Major's face commenced to shed, and words fell out in drools of blue spittle, his flesh peeled back on sheets of wind and fell like raindrops into pools of blue blood. Everyone was going blue, bleeding, and crying blue tears. My arms, my hands, my fingers like tree branches sprouting blue streams. The Major's hair in one fell swoop burst into bright orange flame, arcing out across an orange sky, orange as if a sunset had swallowed it whole. I put my hand to my face and my nose came off in my hand, blue lips impressed upon a blue palm. In a swishhhhhh of orange blue vapor, the Major, Elijah-priest was all gone.

I could feel my ears dribble, dripping off, my eyes leaking out of the sockets, waist deep in a whirl of blue bubble and torrent I was thrashed and spun about. From the heavens came a blue rain, rap, a-pat, tap, and blue stoned hail the likes of hot screaming metal chunks, fi, fo, fum! A murderous raging pain in my chest gashed forth, bone-pierced flesh like the great sea had been parted, and split me in fucking two. "My God," I cried out in slumberous garble. "Take all of me."

Slam, "Fuck!" Into the wall, I'd kicked the dog. Smack! Against the window pane, cast down like a bad, scorned, forlorn angel into the bottom of the dresser, and out across the fuckin' floor. Low crawl, belly drag. I'm fuckin' belly up here now. Awake! Cold with sweat, naked, free, freezing. I'd bruised my head, my fist and rug burns to my knees and chest. My side hurts, and the curtain is torn. It's raining harder now, and the sky splits, flash, spits, rat-a-tat-tat like machine-gun fire. Kerplunk, plunkety, plunk into buckets, drain pipes like blood gutters, bullet holes, buttonholes, and this empty hollow feeling at the pit. I'd been pitted, gutless, so fucking vacant. Whose sins are these? Are we all really dead? What the fuck did Elijah want? And the moon's a grayish hint of blue hue, and shadows by streetlight upon the rain-beaded window glass, silhouette on the wall like black tears. Jesus, where's my blanket? Afraid to sleep anymore, but I need so badly, so bad, to get warm.

Three days back in the world and I'm up before the birds, before the trees, before the sky and branches reaching. Waiting, waiting for the sun to begin, for the heat to come up before I come out from my blanket. A train whistle off in the distance, up the block, two clicks. It ain't that kind of whistle or siren, and the fuckin' streetlight goes out. Again I'm in blue-gray shadow, still waiting. Church bells, and the wind chimes off the back deck. Newsprint hits the front steps, the workings of a bicycle chain. Squawk! A squawking blackbird sounds reveille. I'm an empty Bat-Car, third car from the rear. Three hundred and sixty-five of' em. Stop counting, stop waiting. It's Easter, Easter fucking Sunday! Beyond the torn curtain lace there are only shadow limbs groping for the sky. Other blackbirds squawking now like a party of thieves. Fresh road kill, I heard the brakes an hour ago, screech and thu-thump! Fuckin' Rodney never knew what hit him! *If!* Another fuckin' whistle, another train in the opposite direction.

Me and Jimmy, brothers Don and Jeff, Johnny, Mule, Gonzales, Worm, and Billy Gibbons, us Dick Street Bombers, we played on them tracks. We played war, Get-the-Bag, Kick-the-Can, Hot-Beans. We built forts under the bridge, dammed up the creek, hit homers over the fence, over the rails. We smoked cigarettes, sipped wine, talked sex. We showed each other our dicks, Johnny had the biggest. "You idiot, babies didn't never come from fuckin' storks!"

There are other birds talking now, red, blue, and gray. A coo, cooing mourning dove takes Bight. The rhythmic hammer of that train passing, the heat hiss, hissing up. My cigarette ash falls to my chest. A neighbor's car whines, starts, grinding gears and drives off. I'm safe here, without really thinking, not consciously, but the night's fuckin' over. And again, we get to do it again.

I come out from my blanket, push up from my hands to my feet and stand naked before the window. There are no faces in the glass, but mine; what's only me is scary. We stretch. I'm five-foot-ten and all of 135 pounds. I'm apart, a part of, superimposed upon that tree, without leaves like lines of bark my ribs can be counted. When I left for the war I was 160 and flawless, but the heat, sweat, bad water and food, C-rations, and constant diarrhea made me as thin as a communion wafer, lean like a manhole cover. My eyes sunken-in like a sewer rat's, more black than blue anymore, my face long and narrow and missing teeth. Who is it? It ain't me, these puffs of white steam. Is it breath? Am I breathing? Or am I just a broken limb, a cut branch, kindling for the fire? Is this cover about to blow, and who will receive me?

I put my pajama bottoms on and realize I've put them on backwards. I've stopped pissing out my asshole or I'd be politically correct, could be fuckin' president. I need to make myself laugh, me and God share a laugh. There are no bunkers here, but for an old sparrow's nest under the eaves of shingle next door. I'll go ahead now and turn myself around.

Squirrels padding, pit-pat, pit-pat on the roof above, voices down below. Too much fuckin' TV. The front door creaks, and the screen door grates. My father retrieves the paper, his mumblings about it having blown apart. Yes, I have seen the pieces, bits of brain matter, all pink, and blue, and gray flesh. Just one, one patch. "Jesus," he snaps at my little brother watching cartoons, "Turn it down!" His life's so fuckin' simple: work, drink, eat, drink, sleep. "Let the dog out." Oh, and how he loves his crossword puzzle as he makes his way across the dining room, shuffling pages, into the kitchen, into his coffee cup.

The bathroom is pink and gray tiles, and too fuckin' bright. Kill the light! This piss is freedom, emancipation from one's inner demon: a moment's bliss like a yawn or a sneeze. Only with these bodily functions is there any reprieve. A good dump is king, but for a shot of dope. If! What Casey already knows. I splash some water on my face, but still come back orange. It's that clay, red dirt, those convoys in an open Jeep, too much fucking sun.

My mother's voice rises up from the kitchen, a wafted aroma of coffee, eggs, and bacon, sizzle, pop-pop. No small-arms fire here, just appetites. Mom's cooking will soon enough fatten me up. Only one night we feasted on steak, Shrimp Scampi, Brussels sprouts, my favorite, and wild rice. I had two pieces of strawberry shortcake. "How was it?" she asked, and without thinking I blurted out, "Fucking great! Best fucking meal I ever fuckin' ate!"

My youngest brother and sister, Billy's seven and Marianne's nine, sat there dumbfounded, mouths agape. Everything stopped as if a rock had hit, like someone farted in church, but you'd better not laugh. Shay, eighteen, and John, fifteen, took to snickering; even Dad was holding back a hoot.

"Well," said Mom, attempting to rise above the muzzled snorts, "I'm glad you enjoyed it, but I don't like that word." She tittered, giggled and we all broke loose in wholehearted laughter.

I made my way down the stairway, downstairs, Bugs Bunny askin' "What's up, Doc?" Doc took one tiny piece of shrapnel in the temple sitting on his cot reading a letter from home, just a head above the sandbag line.

If! Nothin' was up, but fucked up, and Doc's world stopped six days short of leaving. Don't mean nothin'! Still I couldn't stop the thoughts, the sleepless nights, the fuckin' nightmares. This wasn't the place I thought home would be, the war hadn't been silenced. Still, I was bored, I missed the goddam excitement, the killing game. This world had no meaning, no life and death consequences. Yeah, it was me who'd changed, everything else was the same only a year older. A year of hell, how could I ever again lie on a beach and tan myself?

I opened the door and stepped from the stairwell into the living room. Marianne was hiding between the upstairs and foyer doorways. Elmer Fudd was about to kill that *cwazy wabbit*. "Boo!" she screamed, this high-pitched screech like a rocket whistles when it's in your lap. I went up like a prizefighter does from an uppercut to the jaw, then down, down for the floorboards, stopped! Stopped myself, than snapped, snapped right the fuck out of myself! She was laughin', God was laughing. I jacked her up off her feet by the threads of her pajama top like a dog would shake a rag-doll in its mouth, pinning her shoulders back up against the wall. Her eyes met my stony-cold, blackened rage! It wasn't her but the enemy I saw.

"Never, never fuckin' do that to me, never! Do you hear me?"

My mother ran in from the kitchen, spatula in hand, waving it like a scepter, a magic wand over a pimply frog, "Put her down! Put her down this minute." There were all kinds of whistles screaming in my head.

"Put her down!" My father's voice reverberated, pinging off walls, and out the back of my brain. He threw his pen and crossword puzzle at me, spilling his coffee. I'm an empty flat-car, third car from the rear. Bones was snapping at my PJ's. "Now!" He bellowed from a safe distance and looked to my mom as if asking, what are we gonna do now?

Billy sat bug-eyed, amused, gawking at me from the couch, this was better than any cartoon, I was cwazier than that fucking wabbit. Tears were streaming down my sister's face. What? This fear, it's mine, I thought, from the depths of the dead and the missing. My God, my God, but couldn't say it. I'd brought the trauma home. I'm the fuckin' enemy here.

2 Poetry

Alan Farrell

Nothing So Bad It's Not Poetry

Poeta nascitur, orator fit. So sings classic not to say classical wisdom: Got to be *born* a poet for the privilege of poking your hand up the Muse's skirt...to take a metaphoric not to say metaphorical tack on this business.

Somewhere around 1963, Karl Shapiro, the noted poet, visits the small college where I'm studying, to "read," as we say, from his "poetry." And so he does. "Love," he tells us, "is a fucking skull."

Not so long after that, perhaps 1966, Allen Ginsberg, the noted poet, visits the university where I'm doing graduate work, to "read," as we say, from *his* "poetry." And so he does. "I am able," he tells us, "at will and alone to achieve sphincter orgasm." To his credit—and to the immense relief of many of us that day—when invited by a wag in the audience to "achieve" one then and there, the bard politely declines.

I've been peddling my clunky insight on poetry to drowsing adolescents for thirty-some years now. And ill enough disposed they are to embrace it. The sturdiest of them will memorize it, attach to it assorted themes, tendencies, modes evidently dear to the professor; the feeblest of them simply pronounce it unfathomable, spend their days sulking in darkness and anger; the boldest of them will now and again ask what *makes* it good...when they really mean to ask why it's *not bad*.

"A poem" says Wallace Stevens (or one of them), "should resist almost successfully the intellect," from which premise, it has seemed to me for some time now the...*contra positive* is it? ... has asserted itself rather at the expense of the original. That is: Anything *not* resisting the intellect must, and for that very reason, *not* be a poem. And...dire corollary: Anything resisting the intellect *must* be a poem. Direr yet: anything resisting the intellect is *worthy* of a poem. The notion inherent in the Greek origin (*poiein*) of our word "poetry," that is language "made" or "made up," that is *un*natural and contrived for special, perhaps hieratic purposes, and that inherent in the Latin original (*versus*) that gives us "verse," that is language "other" and evoking "otherness"...these notions seem to authorize incomprehensibility, incoherence, disjuncture, discombobulation. "A complete disorder is an order," says the above Wallace Stevens (or one of them).

"Seasoned language," says Aristotle, is the mechanism of poetry. "Words," says Goethe, "are like coins: there are golden and silver and, yes...copper." No rules, then. And all words legit. That, good people, leaves a whale of a lotta room for us bozos to maneuver in.

As I look back at my favorite war poems, poems I've learnt in school, I find that—to the extent they meant anything to me—they do so for reasons mostly of form, of structure, of rhyme, of rhythm, of image...of *craft* in *short*. And of *craft...I 'm short. Poeta nascitur,* remember?

I study examples of what is called *Vietvet* or *Namvet* poetry. Woof. It turns out that writing formless, rhymeless, pointless verse is a kind of *therapy*, to which troubled veterans are invited by counselors, advisors, psychiatrists, and other do-gooders ready to lend an ear when a middle-aged burnout decides to blame the shipwreck of his life on the twelve months he spent in Cam Ranh Bay draining crankcases. And here they come: the endless scenettes of dying comrades cradled in the survivor's arms; tousle-head kids laid low in life's prime; druggie interludes beneath the very noses of soulless lifers; sensitive Viets our counterparts, our foes yet brothers; pastoral *nha quê* who happily chopchop rice and boomboom mamasan till us dumb gringos clomp into paradise...and on and on. That's my medium? Incomprehensible gibberish?

"Incomprehensible," of course, reads "hermetic" in the classroom. And students unable to sort out what the hell a Browning or a Mallarmé is talking about have little difficulty in believing that pop-chanteuse Jewel is likewise recondite and...eventually that your Vietvet poet is endowed with the same gift. The incomprehension—worse yet—gets compounded when details of military culture or equipment or lore from Viet Nam combat surface in poems, leaving academic listeners mostly nonplussed... yet oddly persuaded they're in the presence of *authenticity.*

One time a young prof, reading, with all due seriousness, a "Namvet" poem, comes to mention of the city Quang Ngai. He stumbles. I feed him the pronunciation: "Quang Ngai." He comes then to Qui Nhon. "Quang Ngai," I tell him soberly. Then "Tuy Hoa." "Quang Ngai," I say. Another academic reads a "Vietvet" poem relating a fratricidal encounter between Viets and armed GIs. "I pop an AG round into my grenade launcher," the narrator says. "AG round"? There's no "AG round" for that thing. "AG"? There's a flechette round, a smoke round, a white phosphorous round (WP), an anti-personnel round (AP)...and a high explosive round (HE)..."HE"? "AG"? The "narrator" of the poem, the combatant, is illiterate; the "poet," though likely not, has only *heard* the term in barracks chatter...the reader, in the same innocence, simply repeats it, satisfied it's some arcane article of *sermo militaris*...and on and on.

Small potatoes? Maybe. But if the arcana of combat and soldiering gets lost in the confusion of poetic flight and the disconnect between two professions, how much more likely that language mutually misunderstood fails to retrieve other subtleties of insight, of aspiration, of emotion, though the words themselves seem recognizable?

Not many theorists of war poetry, it turns out. And lucky for us. One of them, though, is Herbert Read (spelled differently and no relation to Henry), who peddles what the age calls "Imagism." Its tenets? "The language of common speech...new rhythms as the expression of new moods... absolute freedom in choice of subject..." In a 1918 essay, Read makes claims you'll recognize in the application: "... form determined by the emotion... not an unchanging mould into which any emotion can be poured... the quality of the vision, granted that the expression is adequate. *Corollary:* Rhyme, meter, cadence, alliteration, are various decorative devices to be used as the vision demands and are not formal qualities pre-ordained..." "Lineation is governed by an image or idea...or breaks the syntax at the line-ending for some deliberate effect." Worse yet, Read—and a whole school along with him—oppose the notion of " 'character'... built through 'limitation" ' " to " 'personality'... [where]... the mind surrenders to its environment." ' " Character, he goes on "offers little likelihood of growth," it's "formation being 'moral'... its 'taste' rational rather than aesthetic." Woof. He calls this new order "immediacy" or "lability," "the capacity to change without loss of integrity" and opposes it to "education" or "limitation."

Now, none of my Vietvet buds has read this stuff, but they are aware that lines can be broken off, that rhyme can be dispensed with, that meter is no requirement, that words can be chosen at apparent random, that limit is to be sniffed at. They can see that everywhere in what passes for poetry. And they've been told that putting the words down, spitting the words out, chewing the words over eases the pain...cleanses the guilt...purges the memory. Hey...I can do *that*.

Alan Farrell
February 2006

Preston Hood

Rung Sat

I rappel through the door of the gunship
thinking about someone to love.
On patrol I'm a hunter in the blackness
dozing off, hardened, tired of danger,
I sight the enemy, waist deep in Rung Sat,
muscular legs standing executioner quiet,
black-green smudge & sweat curled on lip.
A snake stops me. I wade ahead,
fall through myself like a stone,
enemy voices passing only meters away,
the backdrop of dark, life's death.
I scan the horizon for movement,
count the bodies across the canal,
wait until they slip into the mud.
My mind is a red-brown blur,
a gauze for the wounded we torture.
What's happening seems not true.

Two hours before dawn the next day, we insert
by chopper, on some Viet Cong farmer's land
to interrogate sympathizers,
& search for the mortar tubes
the NVA shell us with.

We demand revenge:
the smell of rice at the jungle top,
lazy orange mist shifting like smoke.

In low silhouette, we patrol to ambush—
our bodies surrounded by dark—
the shadow of surprise suspended inside us.
Across the trail, wind rips nipper palm,
fear crawling at our feet, a wounded man.

We radio in an airstrike—
the wounded lie with the dying,
the dragged bodies hurried away
disappear into bamboo.

Blood trails along the river
mark a company retreat—
abandoned bombed-out bunkers
shallow graves dug quickly,
brown-uniformed & black-pajamaed bodies,
rice bowls & fish heads—
children half-buried in dirt.
I am a man half in the water, half out;
my legs suck into mud.
My hands hold my head outstretched—
hasten to deliver me among the dead.

Rung Sat: a jungle where the North Vietnamese Army (NVA) and Viet Cong (VC) infiltrated South Vietnam.
Orange Mist: refers to Agent Orange, a chemical defoliant sprayed in Viet Nam, which eventually proved carcinogenic.

Jim Murphy

Scapular

Old Father Kelly with his steel-blue eyes
never smiled, stiffly formal
But, he loved Catholic ritual.
Smelled of incense and altar wine…

Gave each of us altar boys a scapular…

Leather strap
Holding two pictures
Jesus at Gethsemane
On the other side, his most sacred heart.

O sacratissimum cor Iesu'

I wore it around my neck everyday…
middle school…high school
summer jobs…weekend parties
making out…hanging out

Basic Training down South
Radio School in Biloxi
Camp Zama, Japan
Da Nang Air Base…I Corps
Quang Tri City…19th Advisory
Khe Sanh …Marine Combat Base …
…kept me safe…alive…

Jus' didn't help the NVA kid killed a couple clicks from Hill 881…
a grunt brought me his scapular…

It's obvious to me…
His scapular couldn'a come from old Father Kelly

Martin H. Ray

Saigon, 1972

There are things that keep light from life
    like thunder clouds over forests
    and fallen leaves over bleached young shoots
    and the shroud of a war over a people...

Blessed are the clouds that darken the skies
        to renew the blood of the land.
Blessed are the leaves that blanket the earth
        to shelter and nourish its flesh.
Blessed a people of blood and flesh,
    of spirit
        and soul
            and laughs
                and marrow
    numb to the mystery of their shroud
    yet living and loving,
                to illumine the shadow beneath.

Dayl Wise

The Cross of St. Andrew

From South Carolina, Morris our RTO
calls me "my pale-skinned brother."
To rest of recon team, all black,
I'm the "White Rabbit."
told it's a suburban white boy,
scoring drugs downtown.
They liked me, what choice did they have?
I was their squad leader
and mother all rolled into one.

They wore black braided bands on wrists,
they gave me, their cracker, a white one.
In the bush, skin tone becomes irrelevant.
Didn't mean nothing... not really,

Read each others' letters from home.
Spoke of going back to the world,
sports, school,
sex, surviving...
but most talk was food.
Mom's baked beans, corner deli,
breaded channel catfish, grits,
and for me, New York pizza.
Arguing for hours,
almost coming to blows at times.

Descending to LZ Buzzard by chopper,
the mortar platoon below sunbathes,
drinking 3.2 beers under the Confederate battle flag.
It flutters from their radio antenna,
a racist blue cross, white stars, red background.

later their Lt., West Pointer,
Alabama boy, fell, headshot,
a single high-velocity round,
mysterious sniper, never found.

The Stars and Bars removed,
we returned to the bush,
a happier,
tighter team,
for we knew,
and never spoke about it again.

February 14, 2008

Lt: Lieutenant, military officer
LZ: Landing Zone
RTO: Radio Operator

Pinkville, somewhere between LZ Bronco and Quang Ngai City in Quang Ngai province with Col. Donaldson's unit (1969).

3   An Office in Hell

Four men had permanent jobs in the company office on Hill 55. They didn't have to leave company lines or participate in any combat activities. There was the Gunny, a sergeant, and two other men, each of them a corporal. I'd met the Gunny in the field. He'd been on the supply truck that was ambushed, where I'd watched "Bear" die.

He'd led a team of riflemen back to the ambush site and captured two of the responsible VCs. Later that day, I'd kicked one VC prisoner in the face as hard as I could, so hard he flipped over backwards. The Gunny had pulled me aside that day and told me not to do that *ever again.* He then shook my hand and patted me gently on my back.

Gunny had been wounded in the process of capturing them, and was awarded the Purple Heart and Bronze Star medals for his heroism. He was the office "boss." The sergeant was the "supervisor" and as such decided what the others would work on each day.

One of the corporals was assigned the duties of a clerk-typist. He made entries in the Service Record Books of the men in the company, and composed a Daily Unit Diary for headquarters. The other office clerk took care of the incoming and outgoing mail, and other miscellaneous duties.

I envied them. I wanted to be in their shoes, instead of going into battle every day as a Rocket Man (MOS 0351). The clerk-typist was a man named Jenkins. I recognized him as one of the men I had met and served with in boot camp. He looked exactly the same as he did when we graduated. He was healthy and had a relaxed countenance. If he hadn't spent his whole tour in the "rear," excluded from combat, he would have been as wound up as Warnecki and me.

More importantly, Jenkins was a week away from finishing his tour of duty. Jenkins told me that his brother, who joined the Army when he was sent to 'Nam, had orders to go to Saigon. He said the US government policy was to have only one family member in country, and he elected to return home and let his brother serve his country, too. All this didn't matter to me, all I knew was that I had a chance to get out of the field and finish my tour on safer ground.

I chummed it up with him for a half-hour and asked him to show the Gunny my Service Record Book, illustrating my high aptitude scores.

"Could you put in a good word for me? See if they'll consider reassigning me to take your place!"

He said he'd be glad to, but he couldn't guarantee any success. The Sergeant approached me later that day, while I was picking up litter around the office. He asked me if I could still use a typewriter.

"You bet I can, Sergeant!" He gave me a typing test and I managed to average 28 words per minute. He told me that if I wanted a reassignment, I could replace Jenkins and finish my tour working in the company office.

"Hurray!" I shouted.

When the company returned from the field, the Gunny spoke with my platoon leader, Lieutenant Spivey, about my transfer.

I disliked Spivey. He was a tall, thin man and was "full of himself" because he was an officer. Spivey was all of 23 years old, but had a baby face. He had a nasty trait. Occasionally, he snuck up on me, from behind, when I stood night watch. He did that four or five times, and each time it scared me senseless. This added another spike in my already high startle response.

His antics caught up with him eventually and he paid a heavy price for his foolishness. We were on a company-sized operation. It was night and we had set up our perimeter of defense on top of a wooded hill. A machine gun team had been positioned a few meters to my right. They had taped a hand grenade to a tree and strung a tripwire through the firing pin and then secured the other end to an adjacent tree. It was mounted chest-high.

Spivey snuck up on those men, in an attempt to surprise them, and tripped the booby trap. It exploded and severely wounded him on the right side of his head. He was medevac'ed. The Gunny later read us a letter written from the hospital saying he had been blinded; he never returned to the hill.

My transfer was granted. I picked up the rest of my gear from my tent, promoted my A-Gunner to Gunner, and made a home for myself behind a wall that separated the office from my new living quarters. It was May 21st, 1967, a date I would never forget.

I wouldn't have to go out on patrols anymore. I wouldn't have to go out on operations anymore. No more standing watch at night. That's when I started having nightmares about my combat experiences.

When I transferred from the field and into the company office, what I expected to happen didn't happen. I thought I would be greeted with contempt for leaving the combat zone behind. Instead, the men I had stood shoulder-to-shoulder with in combat treated me exactly the same, whether I was "grunting it out" with them on a patrol or handing them their mail from the front door of the company office. I realized that there had been a unique bond established between men who have risked their lives in the same venture.

I value this bond, and will cherish it for the rest of my time here on Earth. Sharing what little we had with each other was a part of that union of spirits. If one man had coffee and the other didn't, the cup would be passed back and forth without a word being spoken.

This sharing sometimes took bizarre turns, like the night a machine gunner I had served with sent a "runner" to my quarters at about 2100 hours. I didn't know the guy who came to get me, but he said "Andy told me to get you to come with me to his bunker. Don't ask questions. Just follow me, Corporal."

I knew Andrew and trusted him. I followed the runner back to a bunker down the left side of the hill. Inside the bunker were Andy and another Marine I didn't know. They were taking turns raping a young Vietnamese woman.

"Powell! I was never selfish with you in the field, and you'd give me the last bullet you had if I asked you for it. Have some of this ass before I blow her away!"

What has this world of mine come to? Do I even know this man?

"Thanks, but no thanks. I appreciate the offer, but I'll be court-martialed if I'm caught out here, doing that, and I can't risk it. What are you going to do with her after you are done?"

"Take her back outside the wire where we found her and grease her. She's a VC Nurse we caught coming back to the hill. She had this coming for a long time."

I grunted my understanding, and then headed back to my cot thinking about the world I was living in and hating every minute of it.

* * *

I didn't make friends with anyone I served with in combat. If I did, (I thought) then I'd worry about them, and if I got distracted like that, either I'd be killed or wounded, or they would be. So, why make friends? I dearly thought this could change after I was transferred into the company office.

There were many injuries we suffered on a daily basis, from gunshots, land mines, Punji stakes, and boobytraps. Somehow, it was easier to accept if it happened to someone I didn't know. I thought friendships would jinx my chances for survival.

I decided that if I got close to someone, I'd begin to worry about their safety. If that happened, the chances were greater that I wouldn't stay focused on saving my own life, and that was not an option for me.

One of my worst experiences actually happened *after* I was assigned to the company office. While I was still in the field, I made a fateful mistake and it cost me dearly, emotionally.

I had returned from a routine patrol early one afternoon. There was a "new guy" in our tent. He was about nineteen years old. He wore a pale green tee-shirt and red Marine Corps swimming trunks.

I looked at him and thought Oh boy, is this guy an innocent, or what?

He returned my stare, gave me a nervous grin, with no teeth showing through his lips. I smiled back.

"Who are you?"

"My name is Kenny Haas. I'm a machine gunner and I just got here."

The latter was obvious. I laughed out loud and said "No kidding, Sherlock!"

I told him my name and that I was with Rockets, showed him around the tent, and assigned him a cot of his own. After he settled in, I gave him a guided tour of the hill so he would know the basics of living there with his and my other tentmates.

Kenny was a very sweet, gentle giant, and I liked him immediately. I took him under my wing and began worrying about his safekeeping while he was in 'Nam.

I knew, however, I'd made a cardinal mistake, for I'd vowed to never make friends in 'Nam.

He had been raised on a farm in Wisconsin along with a passel of siblings. He was used to all sorts of manual labor. Kenny was strong!

One of the daily tasks we did for our tent was to fill four five-gallon cans from a "Water Buffalo," a small tanker towed by the supply truck. We used the water for drinking, shaving, bathing, and cooking.

The Buffalo was two hundred meters up the hill. We'd fill the cans, and carry them back to the tent. Until Kenny showed up, we needed two men to carry the water. Kenny's first turn to get water came up. He grabbed all four cans, got the water, and carried them back. A gallon of

Kenny Haas with his M-60 machine gun. Source: DWP

water weighs around eight pounds so he had about 160 pounds under his arms. He did the work of two men without the slightest hesitation.

Kenny and I became very close. One day, with no patrols for either of us, he started an intimate conversation. "David. You've become a father-like figure to me. Would you please tell me about how you grew up? I'd really like to know more about you."

"Kenny, sure I will, but I'd like to know how you grew up, first. Tell me about your upbringing."

"OK...but there's not much to tell. I'm one of eight kids, the third one born. I have two younger brothers, ages five and six, and the rest are girls. We all live on the family farm and raise cows for milking. From as long as I can remember I helped dad with the chores. I never went to school. Mom gave all of us the schooling she thought we needed to get by in the world. I enlisted in the Corps when Bobby, my younger brother could take over my family chores. That's me, in a nutshell."

I nodded and thanked him for his history, albeit short and simple. I hadn't thought carefully about my younger days before.

"There's not much to tell you about. I was born and raised in Southern California. I lived in East L.A., Long Beach, and now I live in Pasadena. I've got a younger sister. I'm married. Dad is in data processing. I was a computer programmer, back in "The World." I thought I was going to be drafted, so I enlisted in the Corps and ended up here in this tent with you."

Kenny thanked me, and then we broke off our conversation and wrote letters home.

With a heavy heart, I now say to you that Kenny's childlike innocence caught up with him.

I had been in the company office about two months. The security of the bridge over the river, separating the villages to our right from Hill 55, became the responsibility of my company. It had sandbag bunkers on both ends, where men would stand watch.

One evening, at dusk, some VC assaulted the bridge and killed two men. One of dead men was Kenny. The other was Lance Corporal Gutierrez. Gutierrez was a young, married Mexican-American from Southern California.

Gunny ordered me to identify Kenny's remains for positive identification, 'cause I knew him best. I abhorred the task, but I agreed to do it.

Kenny had been sitting on top of the bunker during his watch, heating some hot chocolate over a C-ration stove, when the attack occurred.

He was nearly cut in half with an RPG-7 shoulder-operated rocket, much like an M-72 LAW rocket. I collapsed to my knees and began sobbing uncontrollably when they turned back the tarp and showed me my dead "adoptee."

The blood drained from my brain. I vomited...I fainted. I was revived by a Corpsman, who jammed some smelling salts under my nose.

I had hounded Kenny, constantly, to be vigilant and to protect himself at all times. He forgot, I guess. Maybe he was daydreaming about a happy time in his past. I hope so. How horribly ironic it was that he was killed with a weapon similar to the one I carried when I was in the field.

Lance Corporal Kenneth Daniel Haas (MOS 0331, "Machine Gunner"), formerly of Stanley, Wisconsin, died on August 5th, 1967 at the age of 21 years. The Combat Area Casualties File lists his cause of death as "fatal injury by an explosive device" and duly notes that his body was recovered.

A few weeks had passed since Kenny died and as the mail was being readied for handout, I came across an envelope addressed to "Anybody who knew Kenneth Haas." I was surprised and bewildered. I took the letter out of the stack and stuffed it into my shirt.

This letter is addressed to me. If anyone knew Kenny well, I was first on that list.

After my shift was over I went over to my cot and sat down. I pulled the envelope out of its hiding place and carefully opened it. The letter began:

> Dear friend of Kenneth,
>
> I hope that you can tell us just anything about what happened to my son. Please.
>
> I have asked the Marines about what happened to him, but all they say is that he died in action in Viet Nam, and nothing more. We already knew that after they delivered the news and his Purple Heart on our doorstep that horrible day.
>
> Just anything at all you can tell us would be very much appreciated.
>
> Thank you,
> Kenneth Haas' Mother

I was touched by the simple request, and enraged at the Corps for being so callous about the death of a loved one. I decided to write her a letter that would praise her son, although Kenny had died probably without ever knowing what hit him or that he was in a firefight. I told her that he fought bravely to defend the bridge. In my heart, I know he would have given it his all anyway, if allowed half a chance. Dead is still dead, valiant or no and I just wanted his mom to be proud or at least feel that he died for something.

On September 18th, 1967, Mrs. Haas wrote back to me.

>Dear David,
>
>You will never know how much your letter has ment [sic] to us and that men like you will write such letters trying to comfort us when you men need comforting too. I have heard of the deep friendships that these soldiers make and keep. I don't know quite how, but it seems you have answered our questions without us ever asking them. It did his father good to hear how Kenneth talked of farming as Kenneth was the one who could do the most work of the three oldest boys. Since you wrote to us we have received letters from LCPL David Barclay, Jerry Shehan, and Roy Sprague.
>
>I want to tell you how wonderful I think you boys must be with the fear and hardships and so seldom a word wrote home about them. Only now can I guess at what it must be like to live in this danger and fear. How I wish I might help in some small way.
>
>I just got a call from Minneapolis that they have four medals to present to us. The Purple Heart is one. It is hard to receive them. During our bad time, Kenneth's two older brothers came home and helped were [sic] ever they could, wash dishes, cook, clean, and help Dad with the two little brothers. So please say a few prayers for Kenneth, seven brothers and sisters and a Mom and Dad too.
>
>May god bless you and keep you.
>Kenneth's mother
>Mrs. Melburn Haas
>Stanley, WI, RR1

Life, in "the rear," was infinitely safer. There were no more patrols, no watch to stand, and no more surprise operations to go on. Still, I carried my rifle and ammunition every time I ventured out of the office.

Sergeant Laulu wandered into the office one afternoon. He asked if he had any mail lately. He said he hadn't heard from his family in over three weeks and thought that his letters got hung up in the "system." I told him "No, Sarge, there isn't any undelivered mail for you here." (In retrospect, that was a clue that the folks in the "real world" were distancing themselves from us warriors.)

"Why I didn't get a Purple Heart the day we were ambushed?" I asked.

He said, "I remember the Corpsman patched you up, Powell. How bad were you wounded?"

"Not bad. He rubbed some alcohol over my chest with a cotton swab. My flak jacket absorbed most of the impact, and left me with a little cut across the left side of my ribcage."

"I guess he was paying you back for killing that woman, or something like that. Doc didn't like you very much. I knew he didn't put you in for it, on purpose, but I was waiting to see if you'd ask me about it." He turned around, faced the Gunny, and told him about the incident.

The Gunny was angry! "Sonofabitch! I'll tell the Captain and get this taken care of, Powell. I'm sorry you were disrespected."

I had been working in the company office for six weeks when Gunny's time in country expired. A First Sergeant (nickname: Top) was assigned to replace him and took command of the company office. He was short and fat. I was happy to see the Gunny get out of Viet Nam, yet sad at the same time because he was a good man and I'd miss his friendship.

Top had been transferred to Viet Nam, and to our company, for something he must have done terribly wrong back in the States. I say that because he had been a tuba player in the Marine Corps Band prior to replacing Gunny.

Until his arrival, I enjoyed a modicum of respect for my service in the field. The respect came from the Gunny and the other office men, as well as the men still in the field that knew me. This treatment was horrendously dashed after the Top found out that I was an Infantryman, first, and not a "legitimate" administrative aid. He threw a fit when he reviewed my Service Record Book and saw I was a Grunt.

"What are you doing working in the office! You belong in the field! As soon as another admin man shows up anywhere in the Battalion, he's going to replace you and you're going back where you belong!"

The Top was a cruel, vicious boss. He began every morning the same way. As soon as he strode into the office he would shout out my last name, then issue the same threat.

"Powell!", he bellowed.

"Yes, First Sergeant!"

"Any admin men here yet?"

"No, First Sergeant!"

"Then get to work and find me one!"

I loathed him. I thought he had the authority to send me back to face the dangers that patrols and operations posed. I was scared out of my mind. His abuse of me greatly enhanced my fear and resentment of authority figures.

The Battalion officers finally realized the significance of the problems with the M-16 and subsequently had a makeshift firing range constructed about a hundred meters to the rear of my office. It was put in between the office and the mess hall. It was built just below "street level," which muffled the sporadic gunfire noise.

An admin man showed up at the company in late August. The Top was grinning ear-to-ear! "Get ready to pack up, Powell!"

Instead of replacing me in the company office, he took over Top's duties in the office. This sat well with the Top, but it also proved that the officers in my company had more authority than he did. The Top discontinued his daily taunts, but his smirk whenever he looked at me continued the mental abuse. He also quit coming into the office on a daily basis.

I took the new man over to the mess hall for lunch. We were walking side-by-side, chatting about nothing in particular, when we passed by the rifle range. Suddenly, a few men shot several semi-automatic rifle bursts on the range. I instinctively dived to the ground. The sergeant just stood there looking at me with a wide-eyed stare and a smile across his face. I was humiliated! My startle response reaction was seared even deeper into my subconscious.

In October 1967, I decided to take another R&R. I chose not to go visit my wife Kathy, based in part upon how the first visit had gone when I did see her, and in part based upon how I felt about her after I received those repetitious letters from her. I had spent the previous R&R in a drunken stupor in Honolulu with her and was ashamed that I had forced myself on her more than once. She never quit writing me about her fun times at night and on weekends. I felt like she had been cheating on me!

I had been introduced to Kathy via a 'blind date.' I'd loved Kathy before all this combat stuff, but I had lost that love for her and for my fellow humans, and for myself. Probably her best quality was her honesty. She couldn't tell a lie, even if it was going to hurt her in the long run. In the end, her 'honest' letters *did* hurt her.

Kathy and I tried to have kids right after we were married, but we found out that it would take a miracle for her to get pregnant. She had a medical condition they called something like "endometriosis."

All that history with Kathy was contained in another lifetime.

I went on R&R to Japan. I stayed in a little town outside of Tokyo. I didn't want the crowds or the hustle-bustle of big city life. The R&R lasted seven days. The day before I was scheduled to return, I took a tour offered by the hotel where I stayed. The tour went by train to and from a large lake. Other servicemen were in the travel party.

The sights were beautiful but the train ride back to the hotel area was horrible and mysterious. When the tour group started back to the train station from the boat landing, the tour guide told us all to run to the station as fast as we could. No one stopped to ask why; we took off and didn't stop until we were on the train.

I asked the tour guide, after the train started back down the tracks, why we had to run like that.

"War protesters were headed toward our group, and I didn't want you folks to be exposed to their antics."

That was the first glimpse I had that the participants in the Viet Nam War were unpopular. I went back to Hill 55 and finished my tour, and wondered what kind of reception awaited me back "in the World."

Thoughts about my in-country service haunted my days and nights as I waited to go home. They intruded on my sleep in the form of nightmares. My comrades scared me.

4 Poetry

Alan Farrell

Expended Casings

You break out of that dark wood Dante spoke of and into a clearing. You sense at once that this is a hallowed place. Something sacral has happened here. Sometimes smoke will hang in the air that you can see. Or the odor of it in any event that you can smell. Or the taste, even, owing to the complicity of the olfactory and gustatory. But mostly how you know that men have fought here, that lives have been wagered here—won, maybe, for a while; lost, maybe, for always—is that you feel underfoot the expended casings that litter the jungle floor.

Expended casing. An empty shell, once potent. A core now expended. A detonation has animated inert matter, impelled it, set it in motion. Whether an objective has been reached, a target struck no one can say from the shell casing. Only that its quiescence is an after state, proof of energy once stored, now released and irretrievable. And from the casing alone—its priming gone, its power depleted, its one and only one trajectory launched into that unknown—you have to deduce what's gone on here, what the struggle was about here, what victory was won or ceded here.

Sometimes you find expended casings in a pile. Frenetic passion let loose. Desperation at play. Terror. Ferocity. Exhilaration, even. Someone has fired a whole magazine. Several, maybe. Into a green void, into the darkness, in somber dread of the Unknown and in the futile hope that this Unknown is of a sort to dispel with nitrated cupro-plumbum. Other times, though, you'll find only two or three...perhaps a single expended casing. Mystery. One shot, one kill? And whose shot? And whose kill? Who spotted who first? Who expended that casing? With what effect? And who dragged who off in the end...bloody, bleeding, bled.

The mute witness to these convulsions is a slender tube of still gleaming brass, its insides scorched, black, empty. A soldier will peer, wordless, at a pile of expended casings. Stare idly for the longest time as if to reconstruct in his mind how and why these things came to be this way. He will nudge, ever so gently, the sad little heap of metal with the toe of a scuffed combat boot. He will think. He will remember. He will wonder. Think...how this fight must have come off, what rage emptied these casings, deposed them here. Remember…how he himself has scattered burning brass in clearings, in brakes, in fragrant soil just like this here. Wonder…if like these hollow shells of burnished alloy he has not emptied himself of power, of force, of prime…of hope and of dream and of spirit, to become in the end and for all time, nothing but an expended casing.

Preston Hood

Alive or Dead

No face, no heart, your body has no skin.
No birds to watch. One
carries you away
in its beak across the hot tarmac,
you reinvent yourself, dumb as fossil stone.

Tracer rounds ricochet off the Quonset hut.
No face. The monkey drags off your shadow. No heart.
You have to decide which boys to let die.
The Med-Evac is going down. You
have not yet learned what to do after war?

What triage, what sequence, what wounds,
what boy soldier can wait?
You get through each day one sock at a time,
smoke six cigarettes in two minutes.

You check out the book of names. Alive or dead,
you try & save them all.

Dayl Wise

Walking My Dog While At War

For Molly

A hunter,
killed a rat
that first winter
in the Bronx.
A chicken three years later
in Ulster County.
Alison left
forty dollars in
their mailbox.

Late at night,
everyone asleep
opening up that box
writing of decade's-old demons.
By my side,
looking up
your boxer, pit bull
block-headed face,
your worried look.

In a war many years ago,
another world, life...
men, teenage killers
looked up at me with that same look.
Did they... you love me as a hunter,
top dog, squad leader?

We ate, drank,
pissed and took dumps.
We tracked, patrolled,
pounced and killed.

OK... I'm back, girl.
Get the leash.
Let's close this box,

go out and smell those sweet
Pelham Parkway smells
we both have learned to love.

Stay close my friend,
Let's be *bad*!

Tony Swindell

Suicide in the Jungle

(In the Steps of Siegfried Sassoon)

We knew a happy grunt one time,
Young and green, his cause sublime,
With flag unfurled and crisp salute,
Godless Commies he would shoot,
No doubts for him of what to do,
'Til mortars fell and bullets flew.

In steaming jungle, sick and drugged,
Sucked by leeches, stung by bugs,
Sleepless, exhausted, full of fears,
And aged beyond his tender years,
He hugged a frag, then pulled the pin,
No one spoke his name again.

You spineless bastards, stand and bray,
Cheer soldiers in their deadly play,
Think of that boy, go home and pray
That your kids never go in dire harm's way,
Yeah, those other kids can die today,

They volunteered, didn't they?
They're happy grunts, aren't they?

Richard Levine

Memorial Day

Shot in the chest,
your body inadvertently
shielded me from death.

You fell back, eyes open
but lifeless and far
as two coins staring up
from the bottom of a well.

I knew my second wish,
and my first was already
true—it wasn't me.

You were heavier than
life, when we dragged you
out and across the creek,
two of us, running,

each with a hand under
your underarms. What made you
so heavy that I still carry you,

wondering what these hands
were spared to do?
Thirty-seven years of asking,
and the question has grown

faint as the faint flower
of the moon in the cornflower
blue of a Memorial Day sky,

but there, ever there,
thirsty and deep as any root.

Richard Levine

Home from War

First moments back:

shocking
automatic airport doors

return
to the terminal culture

my uniform
through her eyes, the fawn-face

predators see
from dark hiding; the death

stink
their prey release,

blaming me.
How frightening to be

home from war.

Marc Levy

At Nineteen

The sudden shells plummet like great steel hornets
Eager to bite. After the white bang flash they spit
Sharp poison which digs its way to gardens of flesh.
Our clever bullets tumble through skin and bone—
The invisible wounds painful, death is slow.
The enemy AKs roar out, punch hard, enter, exit
Knock us back. During the attack men slump or
Shoot, I rush forward, rip cloth, find deep wounds
Press merciful white gauze which burns bright red.
Medic! they hail in the swift calligraphy of pain.
I am a hive of mercy. I speak in tongues.
As the medevac lifts I collect their names
In the beat of my heart
My body tattooed a hundred times
The long lines patterned in constant sorrow.
After six months I am old at nineteen.

Published in *Chronogram*, Winter 2007

Marc ("Doc") Levy on patrol in Song Be (1970)

Don Bodey

5 Present Day

Flakes, snow saucers, amble down, like they have a mind and don't want to land. In the streetlight a hundred feet away they float like birds bobbing in small waves. But here, in the forty-watt garage light, they dither in dizzy scribbles, ten feet off the ground. Some hit the old dog's nose and some her filmed-over eyes, but she lies there and looks up as though she isn't missing a thing.

When I say her name, she raises her head and a few flakes coast onto her yellow brows.

Jesus, Seth could be in Iraq in a week.

Except, I'm going to give him a million-dollar wound. I don't want him to come back like I came back from Nam.

The refrigerator whines and the old-water smell of this place passes through the door I'm standing in. The snowfall is thinner. Mary's bathroom light stabs the darkness, a train whistles two miles away, a weak God blowing on a bottle. In Nam, when they asked me what I missed about home, I said a train whistle.

The sparkle of the TV turns nearby snowflakes purple and green for an instant, the dog turns her nose that way. How many times have Seth and I sat in the woods together, watching it snow? I lean against the doorjamb, watch, and rub the silver dollar in my pocket. The markings are all gone, it's thin. My dad was hoeing a potato field, seventy years ago, and got bit by a coral snake but didn't die, so the man told him he earned a whole dollar that day. He carried it forty years and gave it to me when I went to Viet Nam. I flipped it for body-bag duty, sucked on it in fear, kept it in my boot for 400 days, and in my pocket ever since.

The transformer in the alley hums with a different tone through the flakes. Someone in the neighborhood is burning plastic. Mary's TV sends game show laughter out here. Everything I see or hear seems bad.

Everything depends on the hunt. *I remember telling him* about killing animals, explaining the reasons: him as tall as a fencepost when we packed cheese, crackers, radishes, and sat until he had a shot. Little female squirrel the color of dead leaves, in a limb crotch. The sun had broken through and he was asleep against me, gun beside him, cracker crumbs on his cheeks. Woke him up and pointed and he's ready. She tumbled and never moved. He held her by the tail all the way home. Mary cooked it for breakfast.

Taught him to shoot same way my dad taught me. Put a silver dollar on a fence post and use a rifle. He never hit it, but he learned to breathe and squeeze the trigger. They don't tell you that in Boot Camp; they tell you to kill. They were right about that.

When the dog raises up and moves I know she hears Seth's car. I get my cane down and we meet in the driveway. Bigger and stronger than I've ever been, a smile that eats half his face. He picks the dog up like a pillow and her long yellow tail sweeps the air, her tongue searches for his chin. He lays the dog on the car's hood, sweeps the 'phones off his head.

"She lose weight again?"

"Must be down to eighty pounds."

"Mom awake?"

"Getting ready for work. We still hunting?"

"Can't wait." Buries his face in the dog's stomach, lifts her to the ground.

Being in this garage is safe. A thousand nights in this chair, its broken spring pressed against my back. Seth'll be waking up in an hour, daylight another ninety minutes, and the hunt is on. *What do I say?* I'm going to shoot him for my own sake, but how do I explain that?

Electric heater like orange teeth, sound of buzzing flies. Enough warmth for my feet. *Agent Orange.* Millions of gallons into the jungles to eat away their hiding places. Then it got into the rivers we drank out of, into us, and after years began to eat us from the inside. Some guys' liver, stomach, prostrate gland. Mine, so now I wear a diaper.

Throw-rugs on the clothesline wave beyond the dog. Her head is tucked onto her forelegs and she lies there burbling. Each breath flaps the skin of her lips, a burble. *I wonder what color prison diapers are?* When I breathe and squeeze this trigger the bitterness will leave me as, sure as a round leaves a barrel. Forty years of regret in one shot. Emancipation, I'm sure of it.

Trembling a little, and when I get up to walk it off she turns towards me, flips her pancake ears up, quits burbling. A mouse dashes under the lawn mower, starts her nostrils twitching, she shifts her weight, rolling marble eyes.

There is a connection to ritual through guns. Dad and I had our rituals, Nam was full of them, all connected to guns. I was never away from my rifle, knew its serial number, trusted it, depended on it, guarded it. Seth and I have ours too. I didn't touch a gun for twenty years, until he was old enough to hunt. Then I wanted to kill something, or at least to shoot again.

The bathroom light goes off.

I carry my dad's Savage automatic, and when I pick it up, it's like shaking his hand. We hunted a lot when I was young. Never after Nam. Its weight makes me feel like he's here. I break all the rules and all the laws because it's been loaded for forty years. At times I've thought of swallowing its load, but today I feel just the opposite, I have plans for it.

I rack a set of rounds through it and they bounce off the concrete with a *doink*, bring her ears up like gallery targets. Its mechanism is loose and loud, but there's no slop to it. I load Seth's pump and run a set through it too. Tight and quiet, like a new M-16. Sometimes in Nam I wondered who carried mine before I did. There's a grip in that plastic stock that says it's been held, something psychic that says *hello!* You never get away from your gun, so when you come back to the World you feel its absence, and you still think you're going to get killed. *What is that? Cowardice?*

I don't hear him, but she does. Her head jerks towards the house, then her tail wags once, yellow Spanish moss. He's barefooted, carrying his boots, like there is no snow. Piano key smile, ruffled hair, he stands in the doorway and pushes his feet under the dog's belly.

"Here."

He catches it in his boot, dumps it on the dog's back.

"What? Why give it to me?" he says, pulling on a boot.

"In case you need it."

"What for?"

"You need," I say, and look at him quick, "to give it back to me someday."

"If I lose it over there?"

"Even if you don't go."

"You went."

We load the gear, are hardly a mile away when he falls asleep against the window. The road is icing up. The snow, now fine and wet, and the ample moonlight, his rhythmic snoring, this smell of dog in the truck seat, it all seems like part of the ritual. We ride like that for twenty miles. *I'll tell him at breakfast: You get back and know going was the wrong thing for you to do.*

"Did you kill anybody? He leans his elbows on his knees, his forehead on the dash. "I mean, you know, dust 'em?"

He sounds like a boy and all of a sudden I'm calm. I'll hurt him a little bit and he'll be better for it.

"How much of the truth do you want?" It just comes out. "I *tried* to." I raise one finger, "And they *tried* to kill me. I didn't go over there to kill somebody. Maybe that's what's wrong."

We're at the restaurant. He bends to tie his boots. The parking lot is slushy and we lean into the wind. Inside is a bright box, a few tables of hunters. There's a din of talking, the overhead speakers, the dishes banging around, smell of dirty flannel and pancakes. He starts to sit down but I signal to give me that seat.

"Why?" he asks.

"I can see the door. I've got your back."

A chunky busboy begins cleaning the table behind him.

"Nam?" Seth raises his eyebrows. His lips look tight, he suddenly seems older.

"I guess. That's where it started. Anyway, we're going deer hunting."

"I want to know."

"It screwed me up."

"How?"

"That's a long story."

"Tell me."

The busboy moves to another table. He's a good-looking kid, maybe 15 years old. His mother runs the place. Our waitress is a woman as old as I am, who has never hurried in her life. Round face in a scowl, order book in her left hand and that elbow resting on the side of her stomach. She takes our order and goes through the kitchen door. Seth stretches out in the booth and blows smoke rings. My hand shakes when I fiddle a cigarette out. This is the time to talk to him.

"If I tell you about Nam, I have to start with being an F.N.G., when I was your age."

"What's F.N.G.?"

"Fucking New Guy. It's somebody who's never been shot at."

"That's me," he chuckles, "a fucking new guy."

"Well," I hold his eyes, "when I shoot at you out there today, you'll be done with that."

This place was originally a gas station. The front wall is big plate-glass windows, and they are shaking in the wind now, snow coming hard, the faintest distinction of the horizon beyond the snow. Whenever the door opens there's a rush of cold that brings in some snow and blows napkins onto the checkerboard floor. Five guys at the other end of room are laughing, their orange hats like big fishing bobbers. The busboy takes a mop to the tracked-in snow and he's smooth with it, like a dance. I'm waiting to see if Seth heard what I said. I get a smoke ring as big as a doughnut that we both follow until the heat draft scatters it.

"What's it like to get shot at?"

"Depends on whether you know it or not. Could be like hitting one of those homemade things in Iraq."

"Yeah. You'd live in constant fear of hitting one of those, if you went..."

"*If?*"

"Yeah." I act like I'm looking outside for the first time. "That wind is gonna cut us in two, you know?"

The whole room seems noisy when she comes with three plates on one arm, two saucers of toast in her other hand. The gravy sends up a plume of steam, my stomach rattles. This is part of our ritual, breakfast together.

If you go to Iraq, you take a chance on never being involved in love because nobody can love you if you don't love yourself. I'll tell him that after I shoot him. I'm shooting him for love, but I don't need to tell anybody.

My hands are shaking. I try twice before I can get the fork to my mouth. I breathe, look at him, wonder if he sees.

"How old were you when you went, Gramps?"

"Your age."

"Were you scared?"

"Sure. Are you?"

"Yeah."

Since he was a baby, he's always been smiling, or ready to. But now the corners of his mouth are low. He glances at me, then lowers his face to meet his fork. It's odd, for him.

"How's your girl?"

"She's fine," he says. Still looks at his plate and chews. "She's scared too. She doesn't want me to go. She cries about it all the time."

His girlfriend for five years. I can see her round face, big eyes, perfect teeth, a scar the shape of a sickle by one eye.

Now the eastern sky over his shoulder has shifted color. The horizon is something like a TV screen the instant the set is switched off. Hunters from another table pull on jackets and leave, talking about who'll be sitting where. Their conversation fades. My thinking is loud.

"You *don't* have to go."

"You did," he says, real quick.

"That was a mistake I made. Most of my life since then has been tough because of that."

"*Why?*"

"I knew right from wrong when I was drafted. The Army changed all that—Basic Training, Infantry Training, they told me, everything my mom and dad taught was wrong. *Told* me, all day all night for five straight months."

Snow falls into the restaurant lights like a mass of dead moths. I want to get to the woods. I want to shoot him, so he can't go.

"Tell me about being over there, Gramps."

"Hot. Rained all the time. Dirty."

He looks at me out the corner of his eye, gets into his jacket, drops a tip on the table.

We'll do the hunt. I'll shoot him coming out of the woods.

~~~

Ten miles to the woods, past barnyard lights, a dead buck beside the road, antlers in the air. Country music, heater fan whispers against the windshield. The horizon has begun to bleed gray, a line across the white fields like a moustache. Seth lights a cigarette, rides smoking with his window cracked. I can smell the gun oil from the back seat.

I wonder if the old farmer is awake.

The barn has a very small room in it, barely warmed by a kerosene heater we can smell when we pull open the door. He's there, waiting in a chair that looks like home to mice, beat-up faded fabric, it's missing most of one arm.

"Morning."

Wearing a dirty hat with a drawing of a tractor. There's a gap between two bottom teeth big enough to drive the tractor through. His whiskers are a week old. The hair growing in his ears is the color of smoke, but the rest of his hair is new snow. The two ratty coats over a pair of overalls look too new to be his.

"Seen 'em moving?"

"Not much, too warm to rut, I think. Who's this young fella?"

"My grandboy. He's been here before."

"I forgot. I forget everything but how to put my pants on, and mostly don't take them off at night anymore. Piss in a thunder jug like I did growing up." He smiles. "Saves my septic tank a little, wintertime. Lonesome, just me and my cats." Crusted face, think skin barely covering his long jawbones.

Walking towards the woods, the sky light is more than a line, less than a ribbon. No sound but our canvas pants legs and the crunch of boots on snow. He's just a silhouette, a guy walking with his gun ready.

I could shoot now. A twelve-gauge slug is the size of a roll of nickels, pure lead. If I get him in the leg somewhere it'll break the bone. The closer to the barn the better, but I can't let the old man see. I'll let him get ahead of me, halfway across this field, about where we are now. I'll trip, my gun will go off.

The first real color comes on a straight line through a break in the trees, pale blue. My dad was a big, strong man but when I see that blue light I get the feeling that he's here, small, sitting in my lap. Like a cartoon where a guy's conscience is on his shoulder.

Seth and I have talked about how we watch the edge of daybreak spread along the ground. Red squirrels scurry, dance, chatter, bother the peace. A female cardinal moves through the tree tops, the *coo* of ground doves comes and goes like a mantra. Then, a doe and two fawns cross the creek. My heart races. She's big, the fawns are yearlings. If I shoot her they'll hang around awhile, then run away, on their own. She stands a moment, moves enough to put a tree between us, changes direction, stops. The snowflakes and the fawns' spots look about the same size. I tap my barrel on the stand and she's gone, short tail up, a white flag that the fawns follow up the hill.

Train whistle a mile away. The wind stings the tips of my ears, blows cold through my wet diaper. A few brown leaves lie on top of the snow, red squirrel trails scrawl dotted lines from stumps, downed limbs, burrows. I meet Seth's footprints a hundred yards from my tree: giant splotches, evenly spaced. *Never leave perfect tracks again. He'll limp.* If it's not a good shot, he might only leave one footprint.

He's sitting on a stump, orange hat puffed up on his head, gun leaning beside him. A hawk sails the wind at the tree line. The wind finds the hole between my hat and coat, makes my eyes water, bowls into my diaper, feels like my crotch is packed with snow. *Agent Orange.* I finger the trigger, check the safety. My hands are cold, legs shaky. I don't look at him. Fifty feet away I stop. He's looking at me but I don't look at him. I check my trigger housing, where I put my right thumb, the choke setting, the grain pattern in the stock. I feel the gun's weight, its shape.

Through one eye, through the sights, I see him smiling. Then he sits up straighter and his arm moves towards my gun. *Left foot? Right?* His trouser legs get fat above the camouflage boots. One is iced up, like a great big white earring. Target below, the end of his foot.

"What are you doing?"

"Million dollar wound. Hold still."

"Wait!" He gets up.

"Let me put my foot on the stump."

I let a breath out, glide the safety on. Then I switch it back.

"What?" I keep the gun up, but I look at him.

His face looks like it never had a smile. He points at me.

"I want to be the one to say I won't go."

He pulls the silver dollar out, flips it, catches it, repeats. I watch it turn in the air between us. I expect my dad to appear, to snatch it.

His scream comes from somewhere so deep there's no voice to it. From the air itself. I can't look at his foot, to see if I maimed him.

The impact blew it off the stump and the stump is between me and it. Blood coats the jagged top. Some splinters are siren red, blasted back. The snow looks like somebody flung red paint from a brush. He's screaming, trying to breathe so deep too, the scream gets broken into an echo. Arms crossed, he tries to get up from his waist, rolls from side to side on his shoulders, rocking. I throw myself across his arms and chest. He's swallowing his screams like a baby.

I work my way down his legs, still pinning him. Half his boot is blown away, the foot looks whole to the toes. Too much blood, but it isn't important.

I make a tourniquet, use my tracking arrow to wind it tight above the top of his boot. He's puking. I prop his head up; the silver dollar rolls into the puke on his chest, so I clean it in my mouth, then put it back between his chattering teeth.

When he bites, the muscles between his cheeks and jaws get rigid. Both legs twitch. The sun breaks the ridge beam of a barn roof a quarter mile away. The hawk is a feather in the clouds. I smell burning. I put his arms through the sleeves of my coat, tie the sleeves together. Better to drag him that way than to try to carry him.

At first the grain of the wheat stubble defeats me, but I get him moving. The field is level but for a slight drain towards the barn. I walk backwards and pull him by the jacket. After fifty yards I collapse onto my knees.

"I need a gun. Lay still while I run back."

He nods with his eyes open, full of dirt and hunks of straw.

I run. Heavy boots, stubble field. His gun is beside the stump and mine at the edge of the woods.

There's a blood trail along the impression of my dragging him through the snow. No big spots, but every few feet the snow is red on top, a circle the size of an apple. When I get back, I pant and gasp until I can keep my head up.

"Listen: I'm going to empty your gun towards the barn," I warn him. "Maybe the old man will know something is wrong. Don't let it make you jump." I untie the sleeves so he can move his arms.

I pump two quick ones off and they hit just below the barn. Three more, at the other corner. I wait to see if the farmer comes out. Five more, same place. Nothing. He wants to say something.

"Don't talk."

A faded green pickup truck is at the curve of the road half a mile away. We look small out here, if the driver can even see us, over the slight hill. I tug to get going again. I turn around to walk forward, holding the coattail in the small of my back.

All at once it's easier. Then hard. Then easier. I look around. He's raising his good knee to push his heel into the ground. We go on like that, him half-stepping to help when he can. My arm muscles begin to throb and I have to stop. I pant, he pants.

The farmer looks like a child, so far away at the corner of the barn. I drop the sling, wave my arms over my head, yell, then scream. He takes a few steps with his cane, away from us, and disappears behind the barn again.

I start shaking, my whole body like a paint mixer. I clench my arms at my waist and squeeze, but my breath only comes in short bursts. I feel faint.

The tourniquet has stopped the bleeding but turned his foot white. The blood vessels at his ankle bone are as big as a pencil, blue rivers on a white map. Two toes are gone. A *perfect* shot.

"Sthee muh foot," he burbles, and spits the coin loose, before he passes out.

I want to rest, but he's lost a lot of blood by now. *He'll limp. Wear a special shoe, have to explain over and over, live a lie.* When I start again I feel him push us along too, a jerky thrust that becomes part of our slow movement. The old man shows again and raises his cane in the air.

"Help! Goddamn it, help! I shot him!" I try to run towards the barn, but I can't.

The farmer's vanished. It's windy and a lot colder now. No shadow, one star on its way down, over a dead tree with a tire swing tied to a low limb, next to the house. I round the corner. He's leaning against the wall with one hand, and on his cane. For a minute it feels like I am here to help *him.*

"I tripped. Fell." I lie, "and the slug went through his foot. He's bleeding bad. Where's your phone?" He looks like I'm about to attack him. He doesn't understand.

"*Man, my boy's hurt!*"

"Eh?"

This morning he heard all right. He looks far off, but we're two feet from each other. The nearest hospital is forty miles away, but they have a helicopter. *Just the end of his foot. He's okay.* I put my hands below his old chin and look deep into his eyes.

"He is... hurt."

Somebody was shooting at me," he says all at once, "Ten times."

I recognize the thousand-meter stare.

"That was me. Ten shots into the little hill where your barn drops off. Can you hear me?"

"Yup."

Inside, he wants to sit down.

"No. Where's your phone?"

"Don't work. Girl brought me one last week from charity. Dinky little fucker, no cord."

"Where is it?"

One of the cats comes through the door and lands on his lap like a balloon. I squat in front of him, shake his knee a little. His clothes stink. The cat's dandelion eyes watch me. He says the phone is on the table so when I go inside I'm looking for a table. The cupboard doors are all open and the counter is covered by stacks of sacks and cans of food, light bulbs, old jackets. The faucet is dripping into a broken bowl in the gray sink.

The next room is where he lives. A big dirty window with basketball-sized spots where he wipes a hole through the grime. Another barn chair's against the wall, the phone beside it. I go outside and dial 9-1-1. A woman, clear voice, answers. She tells me to slow down, tell her about it.

"Hunting accident. Not hurt bad, but bleeding pretty good. He's in a field. I can't drive to him."

Other voices in the background. The phone reflects my breath. She's typing something. The old man limps to the door, watches me pace in little circles. The hawk flies high, big circles, over where Seth would be.

He is sitting up when I get back, turned around from how I left him, shivering. The bloody sock is lying on his other leg. The foot is mutilated: white again, the dried blood on his pants leg a black knot. I faint. Come-to right away, and I hear a helicopter far off. It's a forty year-old sound; I always hear them before anybody else.

"What's wrong, Gramps? You having a heart attack?"

"I'm okay. You weak?"

The helicopter's a moving speck.

"That's your bird, Seth. They're coming to get you. What happened to your foot?"

For an instant he's confused.

"I was tying my boot and you tripped. Your gun went off."

He lies back and I clean his face. The dollar is on the trail. The helicopter lands about fifty yards away and a man carrying a suitcase gets out. A blonde woman follows him, with a black stretcher, folded in half. The bird throttles down and the blades stop. When I stand up Seth pulls on my pants leg.

"Thanks," he says.

She holds his ankle and the guy wraps the foot, then they put it in a brown Velcroed bag, load him onto the stretcher.

"I'm going to get his mother. We'll be at the hospital in an hour."

They both look at me like I'm stupid.

While they're dressing his foot, I go back for the dollar and when I put it between his teeth the medics look at each other. The jet engine takes a big breath out of the field, there is a high whine, a beautiful sound, and they lift off, swoop immediately and are gone, soon a throbbing spot headed towards the distant amber clouds. The hawk, low over the wood is as big.

The town is small. I drive slow, looking for a phone, before I remember payphones are gone. I notice the inside of the windshield blue from cigarette smoke; the town sidewalks broken up like they haven't been repaired in fifty years; broken glass in an empty lot with three dead trees; heavy *womp womp* of speakers in cars that pass; smell from a gray factory, like burned toast, hanging in the street.

At a drug store a skinny girl tells me there's a phone at the fire station two blocks away, hanging on a rough brick wall. There's a carload of kids at the edge of the parking lot. Our number rings four times.

"Mary?"

"Daddy? What's wrong?"

"Listen …" My mouth is full of the bottom of my throat.

"Why did you call? Where's Seth?"

"He's in the hospital. I tripped…my gun went off. It got him in the foot. He's not bad Mary, not bad."

I expect her to be hysterical but she sounds calm. I can see her leaning against the wall.

"How are you? Are you all right?"

"I'm okay. I'll come get you and we'll go to the hospital."

She is small, good-looking enough to turn heads in the hospital lobby when Mary walks ahead to the information desk. Veteran's hospitals are always full of men waiting. For appointments, prescriptions, test results, a ride, a woman like Mary to walk through. Waiting is a habit bred in the military. I stand behind her looking at everybody else.

"He's in surgery, we have to wait here," she says.

"He'll be okay."

"Daddy, why were you walking with your gun loaded?" Her hazel eyes roam around my face.

"It's a habit, honey. Something I brought back with me." It's all true.

"He was supposed to leave next week."

A stocky man comes out a door behind her and calls a number. Then a guy in a wheelchair that squeaks raises his hand and rolls by us. Two short legs, no knees, pants legs pinned shut, draped over the chair's arms. He's young. The stocky guy greets him and rolls him through the doorway. I hear the chair squeaking until the door shuts itself, then I hear the breathing of the guy sitting beside me. He's asleep

Present Day

and smells like booze. Mary rests one elbow on her leg and holds her head with that hand, holds my hand with her other one. Her hand is tiny. She wraps it around three of my fingers, rubs them with her thumb.

I don't know what I've gotten us into, or out of... He'll be okay. Maybe not play basketball, but even amputees play, on fake legs. Special shoes. He'll get used to lying about it.

The guy beside me is sleeping, boozy breath. He pisses me off, but I envy him.

Mary's grip loosens and she leans against my shoulder. I kiss the top of her head and clench my fists to stifle a sob. I'm going nuts, right here.

He's awake, doped up, face white. I expected the foot to be wrapped in thick bandages, not just looking like it's taped up for a sprained ankle.

Mary takes his hand and kneels beside the bed.

"Daddy told me how it happened."

She says it like I'm not here. He glances my way, but I can't tell anything by his look. He stares for a long time at his mom. Like there's a secret between them. Some smell in this white room reminds me of my own stink. On my way down the hall I begin to wonder what they'll say while I'm gone.

Mary and I sit in the black chairs. Seth sleeps. I wonder if he dreams about it. There's guilt from being close to something big, and there's more guilt from being in the middle of it. Maybe I'll never be able to die, now. I am scared of being an old man scared of living with himself.

Usually, Mary talks a lot, but she's silent now. Sitting with her ankles crossed, her elbow on her knee, chin in her small hand, she looks like she's studying the tile floor. It seems she knows something I don't, when it should be the other way around. She's wearing a necklace of ceramic butterflies and the way it swings from her neck, the butterflies are airborne.

I remember the Monarchs in the valley below us. Our LZ the highest point around. Four companies and Artillery; the mud turning into dust. It was morning. Migrating through the jungle, as if a truce had come, were thousands, hundreds of thousands, tiny agents: orange and black flags, flying across us, through us, everywhere. The fluttering, noisy, cloud of them draped all the way to the valley floor. Everything seemed to stop.

So quiet we could hear their wings paw through the mountain dust. Sound like feather-plucked guitar strings.

6 Poetry

Richard Levine

America's Black Monument

Look at this black wall.
Look how names and years
rise before they fall.
Look at this black roller
coaster, this stone-roster
of death: this black wall.

Already this black wall
is older than the soldiers
whose names it holds. Most are
the names of boys. They died
in red mud and dust, with pimples
and sentimental mustaches, the itch
of longing and close words
on their shedding lips. They died
in rock-beat wet dreams, with plans.
They died trying to kill,
like Orion striding over
the sky after prey, full of longing,
but never surviving the light of day.

Most were boys. They died
naïve. But for each name up
on that black wall, two who
made it home safe have taken
the fall on their own
swords, turned themselves
to stone. What kind of war
claims 56,000 KIAs with more
than 120,000 suicides placed
in monumental unmarked graves?

I was lucky: love pumped life

into the suicide-stone
hanging where I might have blown
a hole. But I have never stopped
crying, dreaming, or thinking
their black names.

I am the sole witness
and survivor to one boy's
turn to stone. I am his shroud
and urn, I am his headstone

and crown, for I was his last
sight and sound. He may be
my last thought. Imagine that.
Even my children
sometimes want to know how far
my stare goes, and how many names
did I know on this black wall.

Look at this black wall.
Look how names and years
rise before they fall.
Look at this black roller
coaster, this stone-roster
of death: this black wall.

Preston Hood

Purgatory

Your life has been brushed black. Blacker than blue, an inventory of no memory, your unspoken poems vaporize in a bomb of smoke. Each word, a ghost to you now, always less luminous than you remember. Your wife has given chase to another with her spiked-crimson tongue. Jealous love with its dark lace around your neck brings you down from everything you once thought was up: the lover's moon, the sun's light. Even your mind tricks you with doubt. Screams over the horizon, & scores of sleepless nights. Suicide bombers drive near; they measure your fear by the clock. Lodged in your beleaguered soul is an improvised explosive device, ticks away at your quiet. You could have been a painting of Jesus, but you are too ashamed to go to your death the way you want. Now say goodbye to the dark night. When your thoughts flow backwards, thousands have been killed...

Richard Levine

Survivor Guilt

It's all that Marley stuff—
Bob, yes, but not the dreaded
one, the dreaded one—
carting all that crap
he'd commerced, and Scrooge
with a chance to face all he was
still carrying. Good thing,
chance, look back along the road
you chose, even the dark, mean,
ragged twists that shriveled your heart.

Good thing Scrooge wasn't in
Viet Nam, where it took two to carry
a poncho-made body-bag,
so whenever you resolve to lay down
your burden, someone might still be
holding up their end. You wouldn't leave
him—literally—holding the bag,
would you? Good man!
Now, you see, this gets carried
until there's no more road.

Dayl Wise

Pop Smoke

Cherry red,
spilling out
of the canister,
bleeding
away from the high grass,
spreading out to be seen from above.

In the distance, chopper noise
to the West, up wind.
The "wop-wop-wop" approaching,
like a swarm of dragonflies,
banking, nose up,
as if to smell our scent;
aromatic cherry red smoke.

We're here below you.
Can you see us?
I can see you all!
Gunner striking a pose,
saw on the ready.

If we, who hunt other men,
the *full timers* on the ground
are the Alpha males,
then you must be the inverse;
feminine air brothers,
coming and calling to punish,
bring us safety.

We're tired and want to go home.
Mother take us back.
Let us suckle on your breast.
Cradle us in your arms.
We've been very bad.

Pop smoke: Setting off a smoke grenade.
Saw: M-60 machine gun

Marc Levy

Peace Time

We gave it names
Like contact,
Movement or
Bringing scunnion.
We psyched ourselves up
Scowling, "Time to kick ass
And take names."
But never talked about
The human beings.
This is how it worked:

They walked into our patrol
Or we walked into theirs
Or we ambushed them
Or they'd ambush us
Or we walked into each other
Or they hit us with mortars
Or overran us with sappers
Or booby-trapped our automatics
Or hit us with sniper fire
Or we called in Arty

Or Arc Light, Blue Max,
Rash or Snoopy.

That's the way it went.
Wait. Engage. Disengage.

Between the contact and kicking ass
Or having our asses kicked was the tension.
It would start small, then build and build
Until we secretly prayed it would happen.

And then we'd walk into them
Or them into us, and so on and such
And the tension would explode
Like sex

And afterward was calm
And we'd be spent.

Days, weeks, nothing would happen,
Then terror, instant and deep
Then relief, like Paradise,
Since the killing was done
And the living had buried
The wounded and dead.
Then it'd start all over again.

That's how it was.
That's how we lived.
Though for some
That's all there was and will be.
And never mind the human beings.

Never mind.

Automatic ambush: Claymore mines detonated by a trip wire
Arty: heavy artillery
Arc Light: B-52 strikes
Bringing scunnion: overwhelming firepower
Blue Max Cobra: gun ship
Rash: a small, heavily armed fixed wing aircraft
Snoopy: a heavily armed modified fixed wing aircraft

Marc Levy and ex-NVA sapper and writer Bao Ninh, Boston (1998)

Dayl Wise

Vietnam Revisited

Central Highlands, 1997
Bringing medical supplies to a hospital in Ha Tan.

A man my age lies on a cot,
his brown face exposed to the wall.
Leg wounds a week old ooze.
A 30 year-old mine went off, I'm told,
he was gathering wood.

I'm asked to take his picture.
He turns with narrowed eyes,
I aim,
focus,
hate fills the lens.
I close my eyes and shoot.

7 Witness to Rape
Tom Skiens

Charlie Company, 4th Battalion 3rd Infantry Regiment, 11th Light infantry Brigade, Americal Division

It was a beautiful, hot, cloudless Southeast Asian day near the end of April 1968. Charlie Company was conducting a Search and Destroy mission 10 to 20 miles southwest of Chu Lai. We were operating between the South China Sea and the jungle-covered mountains to our west. The command group for the company had established a moving CP (Command Post) on a well-used trail.

The designated maneuver platoons and squads were ranging out to the east and west following smaller trails which led to isolated single hooches or groups of hooches. As we moved south a growing column of smoke became visible as if to tell Charlie, "We got Zippos, we be burning your home and killing your livestock." Charlie could determine our direction and rate of march simply by watching the columns of smoke. We were like bullies that taunt our enemies and when the enemy comes and kicks our ass we act surprised. We say things like, "How did they know we were here?"

I hooked up with two Black dudes and a Puerto Rican from first squad of first platoon. This was a cursed squad that had been wiped out two times during our first four months in country. We followed a small partially overgrown trail leading to the east. The trail worked itself through and around several hedgerows and came to a deadend at a manmade clearing approximately forty feet in diameter. The clearing had a hooch and a working garden. Two adults and some small farm animals in the form of pigs, geese, and chickens were living there.

I had been trailing the three grunts and as we entered the opening I moved to a position on the left flank. I took the safety off of my M-16 while taking a very close look at the surrounding vegetation. We were in the middle of an opening that was surrounded by thick brush and tall trees. This would be a great kill zone for Charlie and so a real dumb place for us to be. I was on high alert and ready to go to ground at the first metallic sound or gunshot. By this point in my tour I had perfected the art of concealing my entire body behind a blade of grass. I had done it before to avoid being hit by .51 caliber rounds Charlie was throwing at us from a position on the other side of the Song Tra Khuc river.

Out of the corner of my right eye I detected movement coming from the doorway of the hooch. I heard one of the grunts say, "Let's rape her".

Before those words fully registered another grunt said, "Yeah, let's do it".

I could not believe what was happening. I think I must have frozen in place. This girl, probably military age, kept on walking toward the two much older adults. Most gooks don't speak much grunt and most grunts don't speak much gook. The adults were probably her parents or grandparents, I don't know, but things were going south way too fast.

All three grunts grabbed the gook chick and began dragging her into the hooch. I didn't know what to do. I thought about busting off some rounds but I figured the grunts would cut the chick's throat and kill the two adults. I looked intently at the surrounding vegetation. I was wishing that Charlie was in the bushes. I wished he would kill me and the three grunts.

I would not have fired back. If Charlie was there, then he must kill us, we deserved to die. My eyes drifted back to the faces of the two adults. I was silently mouthing "Fuck me, Fuck me, Fuck me." I dropped the muzzle of my M-16 and tried to give the adults an opportunity to *di di mau* (run).

I started thinking about killing the Americans. Things had gone so far south that I had circled the planet. Fuck me. As I was working on a plan to kill the grunts one of them came out the door of the hooch holding up his pants with one hand and managing his M-16 with the other. I could not work out the plan in my head about what to do. If I killed the grunts, I knew I would spend the rest of my life in prison.

A few minutes later the second grunt came out of the hooch. He was pulling up his pants and fastening his belt. I began to believe God would take care of things. God would blow their sorryass legs off tomorrow with a Bouncing Betty. He would have them die of a sucking chest wound where all they could do was lie in the mud and listen to their life fade away one gurgling bubbling wheezing sucking chest wound sound after the other.

The third grunt came out of the hooch. I did not see a knife or blood stains. I said a small prayer that at least they did not kill her. It is possible the only reason they left her alive was to save her for me. One of the grunts looked at me and said, "It's your turn man." A second grunt chimed in, "Yeah man, we got her warmed up for you. Ha, ha, ha!"

I rejected the offer and moved the muzzle of my weapon from the adult gooks to a spot on the ground between me and the three grunts. The safety was off and my finger was on the trigger... Mamasan and Papasan began wailing as they ran toward the Hooch. *My God, what have we done?* The three grunts were smiling and cracking jokes.

I was hoping that at the very least God would fill these three grunts with a lifetime of guilt and shame and remorse. I don't think God listens to me on these kinds of matters. We began moving back up the trail to the west. I positioned myself last. My safety was still off and my finger was on the trigger.

About 50 yards up the trail at a bend that turned us slightly to the south stood a small private pagoda. The three grunts stopped long enough to light the pagoda on fire. I was pretty sure God was on vacation because he sure as hell was not taking care of my requests.

Needless to say, I never hooked up with these grunts again.

As a result of this one experience I learned to recognize the sounds of rape at a great distance. This is a terrible thing to learn. Over the next two months I would hear this sound on the average of once every third day. Sometimes I would look over at the CO to see if he understood what was happening. I never received any indication he knew or understood.

This event occurred in 1968 and it still has an impact on my attempts to have intimate interpersonal relationships with women. I have been single and alone most of my adult life. I cannot make the first move when it comes to sex. I do not accept suggestive words, actions or looks from a female as consent to have sex. If a female says she wants to have sex I ask her to confirm this verbally several times.

This kind of ruins the moment don't you think?

I cannot wrap my arms around a female because this is a form of restraint and dominance. If a chick wants to leave me I cannot argue or change her mind as this would impose my will on hers. I lost a wife this way. The list goes on and on. I have probably had less sex in my lifetime than most 20 year-olds in America. I wonder about the gook chick who was raped by the three grunts. I wonder how things have turned out in her life? I wonder if the three grunts give a shit?

On this date, in December 2007, I can tell you that I have bought only one videocassette movie my entire life. I bought it, I own it, and I will keep it forever. I have never watched the movie on this cassette and

I don't think I ever will. I saw the original movie once in a theater. The movie is *Casualties of War* (1989) starring Michael J. Fox and Sean Penn. It is about a squad of LRRPs who display the Americal Division patch on their shoulder. They go on patrol and kidnap a Vietnamese female with the intent of abusing her. Michael J. Fox does not rape her and turns the others in. The grunts never spend a day in jail.

In the early 1980s, I joined a rap group headed by an ex-marine that had been blown up and then shot in an all night battle. He humped an M-60 machine gun the Marines called, "a hog". His buddies called him a pig fucker, my e-mail address for him is 'hoghumper'.

In the early 90s, we held a going away party for this ex-Marine, now a shrink, at an abandoned mine up in the hills. Everyone had at least two weapons and there was no chance of running out of ammo. We had made pipe bombs out of PVC, cannon fuse, and black power. I brought out my stash of National Guard acquired booby traps, flares and simulated artillery rounds. We filled the ex-Marine's cannon with so much black powder that it tipped over backward when we touched it off. We also had an endless supply of beer.

By about 0300 everyone in the group had passed out except the ex-Marine, myself and a Wigged Out Viet Nam Combat Vet (WOVCV). The WOVCV told a story about coming up on two Marines in Nam who had staked out and raped a gook chick. They were in the process of cutting her up with their knives. He then killed the two Marines. Their names are now on the Wall. He still carries so much guilt from this that he is self-destructing with booze.

At first light the ex-Marine and I drove off the hill and headed for town. As soon as we started rolling, I ask Dan if he caught what had happened earlier. I said, "His story about killing the two Marines is another piece of my personal trauma. I am not sure how it fits in but at least it tells me there are other possibilities." I ask the ex-Marine Dan, who is a certified mental heath professional and my long time personal shrink, what he thought.

Dan said, "The message is: you, the guy in the movie and the WOVCV all made the best possible decision you could with the information you had available at the time."

After the going-away party, Dan moved 150 miles north to La-Grande, Oregon so he could continue working with veterans. About one year later I joined this group and would make the 300-mile round trip each Tuesday evening. I never clicked with this group. I wanted to deal with things going on in my life as they related to Viet Nam. They wanted to forget about Nam, except to plan a return trip. I wanted no part of that.

One of the Marines in the group had raped several times while in Viet Nam. He told us once that he could not achieve climax unless he had a KA-BAR at the female's throat. He was married for a while once, which brings up some interesting questions. If he needed to rape to achieve climax, did she need to be raped to achieve climax? I don't know and I don't want to know.

The result of all this is, I see a rape and turn it over to God. The movie sees a rape and turns the grunts in but they don't do any time. The WOVCV sees a rape and kills the two grunts. The KA-BAR Marine rapes repeatedly and becomes addicted to the power.

You can talk all the macho shit you want to about what you would have done, but you had to be there to make a call on this one.

8 Poetry

Preston Hood

Boats near Hue, Viet Nam, 1997

The sea: white beach in formless prayer.

Men ready their dugouts:

one man sits in the stern sewing nets;
propped against a wood cross,
a boy braids rope in the bow.

A sail luffs & I imagine these men, their boats,
bobbing in the South China Sea.
Dark clouds shoulder into a gathering storm.

Shift of wind, push of boat.
One false step might trigger a mine
buried beneath their feet during our war.

Richard Levine

Birnam Wood

Sometimes, walking in a wood is
walking in your dreams. For years,

columns of dead, garbed in green, waited
to be buried again; every night. Every

night, in the jungle-fatigued graveyard-wood
where even the trees and grasses were ghosts,

and I, ever the gravedigger, groundskeeper,
target, and host, the blood-bound brother of the dead,

spared my spare life not to sleep that sleep that delivered me
to my own prophesy-limbed Birnam Wood.

But the ghosts, too, needed rest, and the years have taught us
all to sleep, some in stone, but they will never leave me,

nor I them. It was our code, the flagless one
we honored, and honor, allegiant only to each other.

Dayl Wise

The Woods Move

Two clicks out of LZ Lucy
the team breaks.
Lying against our packs,
my Lazy Susan,
weapon across my lap,
safety off.

Weaponless in the Catskills,
sweat pours down
my face, neck…small of back
soaking my shirt, shorts.
At the woodline
   movement to the left.
Another hiker?

Raising my weapon
outside LZ Lucy
sighting in…
why so slow, who aims?

A white tailed doe
maybe her fawn?
Squinting to see my target… no
No…a hiker with her dog
emerges from the woods.
"Great day" she says.
I smile, reply *"Yes it is"*.

The red-headed radio operator appears,
a kid really… toilet paper in hand,
not knowing death was so close.
Lowering my weapon,
"Have a nice dump" I say.
"Sure did, Sarge".
I lift the pack to my knee,
swing it around to my back in one movement,

return to hunt other men.

A good day,
it begins to rain.

———————

LZ: landing zone
click: 1,000 meters (1 kilometer) about 6/10ths of a mile

Jim Murphy

The Great Imprinting Event at Quang Tri City (1968)

(Reminder from Joe Galloway: only 81% of any war story should be true)

I remember learning the term *imprinting*
In Mr. Hunt's science class.
He was a great teacher BUT...
His name was Dick...
not a good thing when you teach 12 & 13 yr.olds

Anyhow...walking from Highway 1 East to the 19th Advisory MAC-V Compound,
I was approached by an old woman who had a platter of eggs...
And they were breaking in front of me...hatching right there by the Citidel, actually a mighty safe place to be born...
so I bought one...100P I believe.

I was the proud motherfather of a baby duckling and all of the responsibilities that go with it...

And I was loved...quacked at for 'even thinking' of not being right there...
Quacked at when hungry...he'd only take food from me...liked the juice off of the ham and lima beans (a concoction that will have to described by someone else's poem)

And I named him Arnie...he followed me all over...I would say Arnie and he'd quack and come running. Everyone loved Arnie...my comm. team, the Marine perimeter unit, the Seabees, the Army advisors...everyone except Capt. Arnholt the CO...and yes, he did waddle...

Now Back to imprinting:
Best described by Nancy Townsend of Acworth, Georgia
DUCKLING sees HUMAN.
DUCKLING is HUMAN.
MOM is HUMAN.
DUCKLING doesn't see other DUCKLINGS.
DUCKLING is only HUMAN.
DUCKLING loves and needs MOM.

DUCKLING grows to be DUCK
DUCK likes HUMANS.
DUCK doesn't mate with DUCKS.
DUCK loves MOM BEST. I was flattered
I had the best duck in Northern I Corps

As Arnie matured it was apparent he was one very special duck. He slept on his own little poncho liner at the foot of my bed and seldom pooped in our hooch, after a little initial discussion...

He preferred several spots outside the concertina about 20 yards from the nearest bunker...

And he was loved by all ...but the one...

Even the generator guy that never bathed was his buddy...this guy thought he was a DJ and he had a full duffle of 45s and a little player and speakers...he and Arnie would spend hours by the big Allison listening to CC Ryder and Gloria and the Young Rascals...Arnie loved 60s rock.. go figure...I was into Motown myself...

Now I had to travel a bit but Arnie had found his duty station so I didn't fear leaving him after awhile...

he respected that I had my job to do...and he had his

...Watch Duck—the Marines actually felt that if Arnie didn't swim out under the concertina and Claymores in the late afternoon sun...then there was a possibility of a rocket or mortar attack or even something a little more personal...

Life was good...out joyriding up to the Marine Base north of the Thach Han River in the comm. team jeep...BBQs...volleyball games with jungle rules ...(again to be described by someone else's poem)

And then it happened. I had to go out to take down our sites on Highway 9...I would be gone for a month...no big deal before I had a child...now was bad.

I came back five weeks later ...waiting to hear my 'glad to see ya' quacks and there was nothing but silence...my guys couldn't make eye contact...he was gone...they were to have protected him...

All there was left was his bed by my rack and over by the compound HQ...a few Army Special Forces and duster mech. dudes had their muffled conversations, with laughter...... about how to make an "orange sauce"...

Let me tell ya something...I know that Arnie is looking over us right now...watching out for us vets ...all except for the Army vets...so if you were Marine Corps, in the Navy or in the Air Force, listen carefully and you can hear Arnie...FTA... quack, quack, FTA!!

100P: a French Indo-China bank note (100 Piastres)
Seabees: Construction Battalions of the United States Navy
HQ: Head Quarters
CO: Commanding Officer
FTA: Fuck the Army

Tony Swindell

Call It Sleep

The nightmares invariably come about 3 a.m. and can be best described as a sense of being wide awake and not dreaming. I can feel and taste fear and experience physical pain, as well as pulses of electricity running through my body. The images are extremely intense, and are pretty much the same from nightmare to nightmare with minor variations. Sometimes I am alone and other times, people I know are with me.

They all start with blinding, silent flashes that create orange and blue spots in my eyes, followed by a series of thick, *basso profundo* thudding sounds that seem to come from deep in the earth itself and move upward into the atmosphere. Soon, the explosions are so close that the sounds are deafening and the ground is shaking beneath me. I feel tiny particles of what seem to be hot sand whipping against my face, and I can feel blood running out of both nostrils, and my ears are ringing and on fire with stabbing pain. I can hear the buzzing sounds of shrapnel in the air from all directions. Around me, the trunks of nearby scrub palm trees are shuddering with shrapnel impacts, and shredded foliage bursts into cascades of greens and browns. Sometimes napalm goes off in front of me, and the heat is searing, and the orange-and-black clouds of fire climb and climb, and seem as if the inferno will tumble over on top of me. The cracks of passing rifle slugs sound like strings of Black Cat firecrackers going off right around my roaring ears. If there is a literal hell, it's here right in front of me.

In one especially bad nightmare, I see a rifle company commander, face purplish and contorted with rage as men are being carried away in their own green ponchos on medevac helicopters, blood, torn clothing and small pieces of body tissue sloshing out from the ends. He confronts a chaplain administering Last Rites to what had once been the CO's executive officer. "You don't need to waste any more useless prayers on us!" the company commander screams, and sprays of spit are flying out of his mouth. "Goddammit, you better start praying for those fuckin' gooks! We're gonna kill ever last fuckin' one of 'em!"

Upon awakening, I frequently vomit or am very nauseated. It's impossible to go back to sleep. Since I live in the country among heavily wooded hills, I stay away from the windows when the moon is bright because of tree lines, a foreboding as if there's something waiting for

Poetry (IV)

me just inside the darkness. I find a dark corner and smoke cigarettes and wait for sunup.

Written in 1991 for Dr. Jonathan Shay at the VA Hospital in Boston, Massachusetts to document symptoms of post-traumatic stress.

Photo credit: Tony Swindell

This photo was taken the morning after a really severe assault on our firebase, LZ Bronco. The sandbags around him were shredded by multiple shrapnel hits.

Alan Farrell

The Man Who Outlived His Lieutenant

Lieutenant and me used to have this, well…kinda argument
About what to do in an ambush
I'd already been in a couple, figure I'm a vet, an *aguerri*, a beenaround
Duck the fuck behint of a tree burn off a mag wait till they get tired
I got more ammo'n they do more time they know
If they mess with me too long I'll call down the *Johnson*

That's a combat man 'ere talkin', sir
Seen the bear an' smelt 'is fur
Shots in anger, C(*ombat*) I(*nfantry*) B(*adge*)
Get in a fight, jus' do like me

Lieutenant he don't see it thataway figures
Somebody fire you up only way to act is get on him
Assault through it on line break it up
Fire and maneuver like in the book
Discipline pree-vails on the field of battle troops get to
thinking all's they gotta do is get shot at, they're not soldiers any more…just targets

That's a combat man 'ere talkin', sir
Seen the bear an' smelt 'is fur
Shots in anger, CIB
Get in a fight, jus' do like me

I say bullshit do love my Lieutenant though bright and curious and tough
> We all do drinks beer with us packs sandbags with us keeps T(*actical*) O(*perations*) C(*enter*) off our back

Wants to do Right and what's more translates that Faith into Act
Cuts square corners like they taught him at V(*iginia*) M(*ilitary*) I(*nstitute*) not because
He has no imagination but because Honor is what keeps this butchery from
Being butchery but he can't sell me Honor…not at the cost of my ass

That's a combat man 'ere talkin', sir
Seen the bear an' smelt 'is fur
Shots in anger, CIB
Get in a fight, jus' do like me

I say I doan wanna be butcher but most of all I doan wanna be the beef
Important to him to be neither but a soldier
Like his Old Man and *his* paratrooper at Normandy teddy bear Captain in the Ardennes
In the end though he pretty much listens to us pretty much

> And don't sell us for nothing and we talk and sweat in the sunwashed dust and shiver in mountain fastness
> And soldier's Honor rarely enough intrudes into the soiled business at hand

That's a combat man 'ere talkin', sir
Seen the bear an' smelt 'is fur
Shots in anger, CIB
Get in a fight, jus' do like me

> We stumblefumblebumble together upthendown Lao mountains
> Curse and laugh and Christ I laughed with him
> Silly futile fatal ironies I'd never laugh at now preposterous paunchy graying Citizen
> And we carrybury our dead a man here firefight there ones and twos
> Yet at each loss he withdraws a little ages a little sages a little talks a little less about
> Honor more about men hurtmen lostmen wastedmen thesemen ourmen more like me

That's a combat man 'ere talkin', sir
Seen the bear an' smelt 'is fur
Shots in anger, CIB
Get in a fight, jus' do like me

> In the six kilometer square grid Lower Left No Bomb Hotel Nine
> A bonetired sweatsoaked *montagnard* snatches a vine from across his face
> Steps out onto a trail threading its way along this ridgeside just
> As a bonetired sweatsoaked P(*athet*) L(*ao*) ambles aimless home
> Infinite moment of locking eyes fumbling fingers
> Rounds crack shattering branches scattering leaves spattering dirt

That's a combat man 'ere talkin', sir
Seen the bear an' smelt 'is fur
Shots in anger, CIB
Get in a fight, jus' do like me

I duck the fuck down burn off a mag wait till they get tired
I got more ammo'n they do more time they know
If they mess with me too long I'll call in the *Johnson*
I'm burrowed deep into the embrace of a fatroot tree
Shelter enough from fire's reach rounds thwack the trunk spike the black soil
Shelter enough from Honor, too

That's a combat man 'ere talkin', sir
Seen the bear an' smelt 'is fur
Shots in anger, CIB
Get in a fight, jus' do like me

But the second I've taken to hide does not end
And somehow it seems that what threatens me comes from back there not up front
Sure enough out of the brush busts Lieutenant piece in one hand grenade in t'other
Bolts past me is that a look is that a look a *look*
Heads right into it Follow Me Aw Jeezus, sir, what're you doin'
You're gonna get

That's a combat man 'ere talkin', sir

Seen the bear an' smelt 'is fur
Shots in anger, CIB
Get in a fight, jus' do like me

Was just a smallish hole and we did what you do
Cleartheairway stopthebleeding sealthewound but before long
Those fingers go bluegray then those lips bluegray then cold
His hand actually goes cold in mine goes cold I cradle him bloodless me tearless
Gentlybutgently turns out Honor can't keep
This butchery from being nothing but butchery I was right after all

That's a combat man 'ere talkin', sir
Seen the bear an' smelt 'is fur
Shots in anger, CIB
Get in a fight, jus' do like me

We wrap my Lieutenant in a ponchomyponcho I was right after all
Carry him on our backs won't lug this man on no pole
Who died on his feet and face to the enemy I
Would have died in a huddle behind a tree face in the dirt

And now surely shall in soiled sheets old man who outlived his Lieutenant
But *right after all*

That's a combat man 'ere talkin', sir
Seen the bear an' smelt 'is fur
Shots in anger, CIB
Get in a fight, jus' do like me

CIB: combat infantry badge. The Army award for serving as an Infantryman in a combat zone for 30 days or more, or for being wounded while serving as an Infantryman in combat.
Montagnard: French term referring to the indigenous peoples of the Central Highlands of Vietnam
Pathet Lao: Laotian equivalent of the Viet Minh and the Viet Cong of Viet Nam

Richard Levine

Mud-Walking

The year I thought
as many words for mud
as it ladled out for boots—
slogging through two-by-two
in long ballistic lines—I prayed.
I prayed when the monsoon surrounded
the moon and tracers shimmered
over the Perfume River, like ghosts
swimming. I prayed when mud-walking
sounded like chest wounds sucking.
Rice tried to be quiet,
clustered in green columns,
like an army in ambush.

Back home the world quaked
where I stepped, unbalanced,
and someone said, "It's over, now."

But for thirty years, the flood
plain of that ghost-river has called
me, like a bell buoy through thick fog.
I have navigated its night-shade
tides. I've watched it carry people away,
like kites swelled with wind, high
over the delta, the strings strung out
far, beyond any way back.
I've even seen—through the muddy, conical
glow of a Brooklyn streetlight—
rain turn to rice.

Marc Levy

9 How Stevie Nearly Lost the War

The war, Stevie is told, with its white-tailed rockets and hard crack ricochets; the war, with its thumping whirl of trembling choppers; the war, with its shirtless gun crews manning steel wheeled cannons; the war, with its fine plumed shells cutting silver arcs through infinite sky; the war, with its lumbering tanks and sun bleached bunkers; the war, with its steep, lush highlands, emerald lattice of checkerboard paddies; the war, with its mangled torsos triaged too late; the war, he is told on scheduled clinic days, had ended quite some time ago.

Stevie sits on the bare floor in the center of his nine by nine studio apartment; it is a good thing to do. Long past midnight, seated cross-legged, facing the solitary open window opposite his computer and metal file cabinet, he leans against his white book case and recalls the soft patter of rain on tropical wood, the curling trickle of thin, incessant rivulets. In tropical forests before first light, all sound felt amplified, organic. Yet nothing happened; nothing of consequence.

Years later, he regretted that while angry young men wearing torn battle fatigues, unit patches, mud-slicked boonie hats, hurled their combat medals onto capitol steps—some weeping, others shouting, yet strangely peaceful in their rude dissent—Stevie lay snug beneath an olive-drab stockade blanket, thin, exhausted, hair close-cut, unable to attend.

Soon he will rise to make toast, the preferred meal of day or night. For now, Stevie thinks of Cindy's last letter, and Cindy herself. She is short, of medium build, with auburn hair and alluring, firm calves. Of particular note is the manner in which her mouth seems to push forward, as though a permanent kiss strained her curious face. She is pretty, but not in the conventional sense. He had known her in passing, knew his curious manner did not unnerve her. She read well in public. Her writing was better than most encountered at café readings. When Stevie read about war, not once in two years did Cindy look away. Stevie remembers their only date.

"Would you like to go out sometime?"

"Sure," she said.

The very next afternoon they walked for hours in the lush wood of a nearby state park. Toward evening, they returned to Cindy's well-kept house.

"You can come in. I trust you," she said.

Her home was filled with fine antique furniture exquisitely placed. The walls were earth toned, adorned with Audubon prints. The carpeting was soft and thick, rich with patterns of amber and blue. They sat on a plush white loveseat.

"This is Sasha," Cindy beamed.

Stevie gently stroked the calm, beige cat behind its scarred left ear. When the trustful creature tired of his touch, it jumped from his lap and scurried away. Then Stevie kissed Cindy. Simply kissed her full on the mouth. His tongue wandered, his fingertips traveled beneath her red silk sweater. She pulled him, pressed herself tight against his torso, then murmured, "Do you want to?"

And Stevie said, "No."

(Because he did not wish to fuck her like Bride would have. Sharing a foxhole, Bride regaled Stevie with prodigious stories of sexual conquest. Seventy women. Found. Fucked. Forgotten. Then a single shot rang out and the burley sergeant slumped forward, dark blood gathering beneath his head. When the sniper was caught the platoon butchered her. Stevie held her down).

"It won't work, Cindy. We'll end up hating each other. I know it," he said.

He never spoke this way: polite, casual, comforting.

"What do you want?" she said, straightening her clothes.

She was lovely, he thought. So lovely.

"Just be my friend. Will you be my friend?"

When Cindy said "Yes" Stevie wept susurrant tears.

"Why are you crying, Stevie?"

"I don't know," he said. "I don't know."

She held him close until his time came to leave.

In one seamless arc Stevie rises and seats himself at his computer, a mongrel stitched from the wreckage of other people's lives. It is late. The perfect time to write Cindy, who must be sleeping.

Subject: Memo Day
Date: Tuesday 30 May 2001 3am
From: silverspartan
To: mimsypearl

> The Memorial Day service went well. They played the Billy Joel song with chopper blades in the background. No caffeine in your blood, that'll wake you up. Old men read poems about duty, honor, that sort of thing. The crowd loved it. Then it's my turn. I tell them things they need to hear. A few vets said, "You tell it real, brother. Got any more?" But my head was splitting so I left. Petra the acupuncturist thinks it's psychosomatic. Stuck me twenty-one times. I'll wait a few days, see my doctor.

Stevie clicks "Send," logs off, pushes the chair back, decides to make toast. He uses his incomparable, outlandishly priced, Made in Spain, NAFTA approved, Krups fool-proof ("Fuckin doofus proof,' as Sgt. Bride would say. Bride, shot so impeccably), deluxe, white-toned, smooth-shelled, quite nearly noiseless, two-slice toaster. Stevie twists open the plastic bread sack, daintily drops one slice into the left slot, one into the right.

"Yes, sir," he says, saluting the phantom white refrigerator. "It's a wonderful toaster. IT'S A FUCKING PERFECT TOASTER. IT'S THE MOST BEAUTIFUL FUCKIN TOASTER OF ALL FUCKIN TIME."

Pressing the plastic "Start" bar, Stevie beholds the filament rods heating to brilliant red. Six times, in tight three minute intervals, the caramelized shards spring up. Six times Stevie flinches. It is a good meal. A simple meal. Wolfed down in seconds. Stevie sweeps the crumbs off the kitchen counter with the ridge of his palm, then flicks off the kitchen light. When he lies down to sleep, his dreams are not pleasant.

At dawn he gathers up the crimson blanket which lay heaped on the floor. *Bunch up! Bunch up! Like ghosts! Don't bunch up! Don't!* He makes his bed, hurling sheets forward, folding neat hospital corners, doubling the blanket back four inches over itself, tight-tucking neat square edges all the way round. After dressing, Stevie sits at the computer and boots up. Cindy has written.

> **Subject: Acupuncture**
> **Date: 30 May 2001 6am**
> **From: mimsypearl**
> **To: silverspartan**
> It might be related to Memorial Day...duh! See your doctor! It's beautiful outside. Have you been out? Beautiful.

Stevie snickers to himself. She certainly is good at that. Rubbing in salt, licking it off. *Bitch!* May is a cruel month for Stevie. He can tell from his dreams.

Subject: Sleepless and Counting
Date: Tuesday 30 May 2001 6:21am
From: silverspartan
To: mimsypearl
It never occurred to me to add one plus one. When you're the center of the storm it's hard to know what coast is where. Go easy, Fraulein. Here's a dream I had.

Stevie hunts down one of many nightmare files, pastes text to body. He marvels how the mind's inner logic has captured his feelings. Would she understand? He trusts Cindy, enjoys her carefree nature, though she does not yet know about the letter sent home or weekly visits to Doctor Foster.

"0900 HOURS. TIME TO MAKE THE DOUGHNUTS," Stevie shouts, heading toward the bathroom.

Toilet, tub, sink. He pinches a sweet white worm onto frayed plastic bristles, shoves the angled stick into his "O" shaped mouth. Pumping the brush forward and back, foam and spittle streaking his chin, Stevie spits, then reads aloud the framed, aging letter, reclaimed after they died, now poised above the medicine cabinet:

"Dear Folks,
   Today was a good day. We came up to this hooch and a dink ran out. I emptied a whole magazine into that cocksucker. They don't bleed much, you know. Little fucker had a Smith & Wesson. My Lieutenant let me keep it. That's three dinks I've killed so far. Every one I kill I send something home. Last one had a slingshot, remember? Well, be good. Love, Stevie."

Stevie observes himself in the spit-stained mirror. Born mid-century, he has aged well, though his once thick, blonde hair, now gray, receded, he wears neatly trimmed and combed straight back. His eyes, perhaps slightly recessed, hinting at skull, retain their fierce, inscrutable gaze. An ordinary nose, sliced by shrapnel, fits the center of his still youthful face. His cheeks remain angular and smooth, above a strong jaw unjowled by time. Soft pleasant lips perch over a firm, manly chin. Yet despite this appealing countenance, dark clouds swarm across his face, inhabiting his soul.

"Be good... Be good," Stevie mutters, then thrusts his tongue out, rolls his eyes, pivots his head left, right, left, and screams, "MOTHERFUCKAHHH!"

He spits, rinses, backhand wipes his mouth again and again, until the harsh voice grows weak and the reflected image, swollen by tears, abruptly departs.

The monitor has turned pitch black. It is the perfect screen saver. It is the all-time, hands-down, bunker-busting, world's best screen saver. Stevie nudges the machine back to life. After dialing up, he surfs war's history. He pores over colorful maps, imagines helmeted foot soldiers tramping uphill, feels hot kicked wind rushing over his face, hears pounding hooves thudding hard-packed earth, tingles with the absolute delirium of unbridled power wielded by consummate force. It is the perfect way to spend an afternoon. He ducks his head down, wings up one shoulder, wipes sweat from his brow.

"Break time," he trumpets to Spartan emptiness.

> **Subject: Round 2**
> **Date: 30 May 2001 4pm**
> **From: Mimsypearl**
> **To: Silverspartan**
> Your dream was vivid, haunting. Did you ever get the Purple Heart? What's an M-79? I hope you're feeling better.

Stevie reads the letter twice, three times. His emotions choke at the base of his neck. Chess. Now there was a game. A man's game. The salutary compression of flesh and bone redeemed to bantam ranks on rival squares. Duchamp played, as did Beckett. After Hiroshima, Oppenheimer quit. For Stevie, the modern variant, the aptly named five-minute blitz, in street parlance "speed chess," (so well-detailed by K. Ryan in her factual, somewhat over-citationed doctoral thesis, *Outcomes of Antiquity as Applied to Game Theory and Modern Culture*, Michigan State, 1989, available at http://gametime.ms.edu) truly captivates him, so much so that he has spent considerable time and not immodest sums on obscure theoretic journals, newsletters, closed-cable tournament fees, a thicket of pamphlets, a forest of books. Yes, it is the sight of men (for it is mostly men, and mostly ex-convicts) seated on park benches, hunched over plinth-like tables, the boxy checkered squares dimmed by constant use, the nimble Staunton pieces ever ready to fly, leap, excitedly pounce. It is the mere sight of this static battlefield, this perfect simulacrum, the mobilization of varied pieces for clear and calculable ends, which invigorates Stevie, titillates him, brings him no end of cerebral pleasure. Oh, those Greeks and Persians. How quaint of us. How American of them. Was it not Philidor who said, "Pawns are the soul of chess."

The game begins with lesser pieces amply deployed. Thereafter, keenly circling central squares, each player accelerating the swift one-hand-glide to clock and back, cat-like flanking pawns crawl forward, slow stalking knights advance in cruel L-shaped ambush, rooks appear at sudden King side castles, inscrutable bishops discreetly leer. By mid-game, major pieces spar and slug, rain down sequential hammer blows, unfurl violent exchanges, kick and caterwaul, time stealing past on the spring wound clocks.

"Touch! Touch!" a young, excitable player shouts, snatching a blundered piece, the grand queen helpless, pinned to her King by a stealthy rook. This same player will soon survey his imminent loss.

"One more?" the superior player coyly asks, pocketing money.

Stevie has long admired the experienced men who serenely crush innocent, unsuspecting passers-by, curiosity seekers, the novices or merely maladroit who are their bread and butter. Observing expert players, he thrills at exquisite displays of staggering force, hard-won positions blown full backwards, punched through, without mercy over-run. He revels in shouted staccatos of profane wit, prides himself on seeing four moves deep, spotting clever, well-concealed traps, breath-taking swindles, the well-sprung mate. Yet despite his considerable mastery of gambits, tempo, king's opposition, preferring a Caro-Kann to Alkehine's insidious ploys, endeared as he is to Capablanca's mid-game brilliancies, ever appreciative of Lasker's quixotic end game push-shove-push, Stevie remains deeply puzzled. Most fear to attempt what he most admires: the audacity to risk decisive advance without benefit of logic. For Stevie, this secret fear lays tooled by the fine quill of experience deep in the chambers of his heart.

He must write Cindy. A kind letter, Foster would have said. An informative letter.

**Subject: Pawn to Queen
Date: 30 May 2001 11:55pm
From: silverspartan
To: mimsypearl**
Was wondering what you thought about the Sicilian Defense. 1...c5 is the most popular alternative to 1...e5. As soon as White plays d4, Black exchanges the c-Pawn for the d-Pawn. What would you do

next? 2. Nc3. 2. Nf3. 2. c3 or 2. d4. Then of course there's the She-veningen Variation. Or maybe there is no defense.

He would wait for her response. Maybe he could sleep…

At the first high pitched electronic ring, Stevie startles awake. He presses the black plastic phone to his ear.

"Cindy?"

"Good evening, Sir. Are you the breadwinner of the house?"

She is young, naive.

"Are you shitting me?"

"I…I beg your pardon?"

"Don't beg. Just get to the goddamn point."

There is a brief, unhealthy silence.

"Sir, if I can have a minute of your time…"

Stevie's words jet from his mouth like thunderous out-going shells, like sleek napalm canisters spinning through air, like the pure *pop pop pop* of forty mike mike grenades fired by Cobras going in for the kill.

"This is Silverspartan three-six Indy. The perimeter is secure. My sitreps are negative at this time. How do you copy, over?"

She would say, "I read you Loud and Clear," or "Got you Lucky Chucky." She would say, "Thank you much. Out."

"Sir. Sir, are you the breadwinner…"

"I SAID MY SITREPS ARE NEGATIVE ARE YOU FUCKIN DEAF?"

Stevie slams the phone down. Hands in his lap, his eye lids fold shut. I'm praying to you, Father. I'm praying. Protect me from invisible forces. Protect me. Father, I'm afraid. Hold me. Give me your strength. Guide me with love. I'm praying to you. Heal me, Father. Heal me. This is how he prays.

For several minutes Stevie sits unnaturally still. He finds the darkness pleasant and lets himself drift to the week before last:

Once seated, he had routinely scanned Foster's soft-lit cubicle. At eye level a dozen gold-stamped diplomas secure the right side wall, their frames discreetly screwed in place. To the left, pastel museum posters depict flowery gardens, pastoral landscapes, bright-colored boats moored in calm, tranquil water. Scattered across the center, a collection of combat photographs: gaunt-eyed grunts perched in trembling choppers; a sad, weary platoon returned from patrol; an aerial photograph, the grim American firebase desolate, abandoned; a youthful David Foster, full-haired, clean-shaven, thirty pounds lighter, three rows of medals affixed to his chest. Desk. Lamp. Cabinet. The patient's chair is solid and strong.

"How was your week?" said Foster.

Week? Stevie longed to relive his curative past. Yes, the gray fading glory whose dumb stones speak in energetic tongues the anatomy of war. The symmetry of his words, like the hard steely roll of linked tank treads crush all in their path. His voice is pure, caustic, relentless, using third-person singular, as if he were someone else:

Second day Ft. Devens, First Sergeant says, "Where you think you're going?" Stevie heading out the barracks door.

"What's it look like, fat boy? Stevie won't pull guard duty. See you in three days."

Stevie returns, they bust him in rank. A cook wakes him. "Get up. You got KP."

Stevie says, "I don't pull KP."

Cook says, "They'll court martial your ass."

Stevie says, "Good. Who gives a fuck? I just want out."

Yes, when Stevie talks to Foster, his words burn like the bright, hissing pendulous swing of magnesium flares, explode like the sharp *BOOMCRACKBOOM* of direct cannon-shell fire, eject like desperate pilots strapped to cold metal chairs who must soon evade enemy capture:

No KP, no haircuts, no saluting. They hated him. Hated him for going up the chain-of-command. "Stevie to see Lieutenant Carter. Stevie to see Major Hitchens, please. Stevie to see Colonel Olecki."

Colonel says, "Why are you making all this trouble, son?"

Stevie says, "Just want out, sir. Out of the Army."

Olecki eye balls Stevie's Cav patch, Combat Medic Badge, other stuff.

"You Cav boys think you're hot shit, don't you?" He tells Stevie, "Straighten up, son, or I will personally court martial your ass." The dumb fuck.

Stevie's Army lawyer waits for him but an MP ejects him from JAG.

Stevie says, "You can't do that."

MP says, "Get a fuckin hair cut you piece of shit." Stevie's hair is so long his cunt cap slides off his head.

Stevie hauls ass to the Inspector General. "I'm being court-martialed, sir. I've been denied my right-to-counsel." BOOM!

"I'll look into it," he says. "I'll certainly will look into it."

Stevie is chewed out, restricted to base, put on garbage detail.

A lifer pays him a visit. "Sign here. Bad Conduct Discharge. Isn't that what you want?" But Stevie is smart. He has found himself a slick civilian lawyer. "No thanks," he says. "Court martial me."

A week later Stevie sees the base head honcho, General Richard R Shultz. His aide-de-camp says, "The general isn't seeing anyone today. GET THE FUCK OUT." He really said that. Get the fuck out!"

At the court martial...

Stevie lowered his head, pinched the space above his irregular nose.

"Six months hard labor, Dishonorable Discharge," Stevie said to Foster.

Stevie had attempted laughter, but fell silent. Silent, like the fatal dead calm between incoming shells, like the shocked-out point man returning from morning patrol, like the thick metal gears of shot-down Cobras scattered in jungle heavy with rain.

"What's most bothering you?" Foster inquired.

And Stevie blurted out the single word "Cambodia."

"What about Cambodia?" Foster said.

"May is Cambodia. Every goddamn year."

He looked inward. Felt salty drops crawl down his face.

BOOM! They had waited, blown the mines, fired their weapons, advanced when the howling stopped. The perforated dead, not yet transfigured, lay sprawled in waxy tableaux.

"Lieutenant Gill yells, "Chieu Hoi!" but the dink swings his AK up and the LT wastes him point-blank, the machine-gunner blows his head off. I mean you can look down his fuckin neck, his fuckin spinal column, count the fuckin vertebrae for Christ's sake."

"Then what?"

Stevie paused. His voice went low.

We scavenge the bodies, march, set up an NDP. Lieutenant Gill is holding his jaw like it hurts. "It's nothing, sir. Nothing. You'll be all right."

"Purple Heart," he says. "Doc, you gonna put me in for the Purple Heart?"

Stevie says, "Are you shitting me, Lieutenant? Are you shitting me? It's just skull fragments from the dead dink. You didn't get shot. You didn't get hit. No way I'm putting you in for a medal, sir. No fuckin way."

Foster repeated his question when Stevie failed to respond. "What else?

Two months later Stevie's replacement is dead, half the platoon wasted, but he is safe dragging fifty-five gallon drums from LZ mortar box shitters. He pours diesel, chucks trip flares, stirs the shit soup with a ten foot pole until it's burned down to ash. "What'cha doing, Doc?"

The artillery crews can't believe it. "Burning shit?" Assholes! But Stevie is short. Twenty-three and a wake up.

Then a lifer says, "Get your gear. Charlie Company needs a medic."

Stevie says, "No way. No fuckin way." Until a Major with a grease gun says, "Do it."

Immediately Foster asked the dumbest question of all fuckin time. "What were you feeling?"

Stevie burst out laughing, then spoke:

"Stevie grabs his weapon, frags, helmet, pack, walks to the chopper pad. The door gunner yells, "Hop the fuck in!" But Stevie doesn't move.

They sky up. Second bird, Stevie says, "Quan Loi?"

"Yeah. Get on. Get on." *Fifteen minutes later he jumps off, walks to battalion. He knows who gave the order.*

It happened quickly. From ten meters Stevie pushed the safety switch to Full Automatic. "ARE YOU SENDING STEVIE OUT? MOTHER-FUCKER! ARE YOU SENDING HIM OUT?'

The new medical officer raised both hands over his head. "It was a mistake. I'll send someone else. You don't have to go."

Stevie walked straight past that prick, that PRICK, threw down his gear...

Foster asked, "Who's Stevie?"

When Stevie stopped sobbing, Foster said, "You're chasing ghosts. You don't need them anymore."

Waiting for the Internet connection, Stevie sifts through old letters Cindy has sent. He scans whole pages, skips entire paragraphs, rifles an entire year of correspondence, settles on Sasha.

Subject: Sasha
Date: 5 December 1998 8:32am
From: mimsypearl
To: silverspartan

I had to have Sasha put down last night. yesterday morning i took her to the vet because she wasn't eating. he said she was in kidney failure. did a sonogram that showed a tumor on the urethra. i asked what are her chances if we do surgery. he said, "about zero". i said i wanted to take her home to spend one more night with me. couldn't

> he sedate her? he said yes, but she'd be sedated and uncomfortable. i asked how come she wasn't crying if she was in pain. he said animals hunker down, find the dark, keep quiet when they're hurt. otherwise might be hunted down. i looked into her eyes. she looked at me then looked away. i held her. she weighed 5.8 lbs, down from 7.6 a couple of months ago. i wanted to scream. i asked him if he was staying late just for this. he shrugged his shoulders. i signed the papers. he gave her something to make her go slowly asleep and left me alone with her. i could feel her weight sag. i didn't know what to do. i just stood there holding her. finally he came back in and gave her the injection. the nurse had to come in. i asked why. he said to hold her. but she wasn't moving. the nurse asked me if i was ok. i said "no". then they left me alone with her again. she was heavy. her head bobbed. i didn't know what to do. finally they came back. i said i wanted to take the body and bring it back the next day so they could cremate her. they said it was hot. not a good idea. but ok if i wanted to. i went back in and looked at her eyes. she wasn't there. so i walked out and said never mind—i don't want the body. they said will you be alright driving home by yourself. i said i don't know. i stopped to buy gas on the way home. the attendant came out because i couldn't figure out where to put the credit card, how to put the nozzle in. the guy got annoyed, did everything for me. i said i had just had my cat put to sleep. he said the gas prices were actually higher than shown and started to change the signs. I'm sitting here in my apt and sasha is everywhere. and nowhere.

It was a good letter. A wonderful letter. Sincere and heartfelt. Stevie loved her. Even if she couldn't understand what drove him, uncoiled him, what each day drove transformed men to shoot and shoot, or shake with fear, or cry out from perfidious, improvident wounds, or seek revenge, yes, grow accustomed to it, yes, love it, yes, the bloodlust killing, search and find them, yes, hunt them down like dogs, they are hunting too, yes, do you understand, Cindy, they are hunting and we are hunting. Oh Cindy, yes, yes, was it not ever so: we hunted and killed each other in order to survive. My dearest, dearest sweet and lovely Cindy was it not Pindar's fate to render in hard set stone, "Oh passerby, go tell the Spartan's we lie here in obedience to their laws."

Sweet, dulcet, simple Cindy. She had lost her cat. Her dumb-fuck shit-ass cat. Heat rushed to Stevie's face. Rockets, mortars, ambush, monsoon. We lived and loved and killed like dogs. Don't you get it? Oh, Christ. Oh, Cindy. Oh, passerby. Yes, we lay down like obedient dogs.

Yes, my darling Cindy who dares to listen, who does not turn away, who remains ever faithful, Cindy of the ever fuckin-stupid questions, yes, so ever stupid I want to choke you, choke you, yes, yes, I want to slit your throat, just once, straight across, see fresh blood spurt in spiraled beats across your well kept home. Oh loving, lovely Cindy, who cares for Stevie, accepts him, does not turn her back, or shy away, or make unkind remarks: what do you know about death? What? And what do you know about war? Stevie flinched. No. NO. He pummeled and struck ever widening circles in callous, empty air. It was not possible. He would not allow it. Foster could not be right.

Overwhelmed, Stevie lay down beneath the red blanket, sunk his face into a yielding white cloud and curled himself to sleep. In the dream, he made love to her. Long, full, luxuriant love. Afterwards, he drew himself over her, dotted sweet kisses across her luminous mouth. "I'm kissing you, Cindy," his dream-self said.

He woke as usual, as if suddenly tugged. The cooling fan whirred inside the computer. Its black plastic fins recalled spent mortar shells poking out from dry blasted earth. Delayed fuse, direct impact, dread aerial burst, each had its fearful effect. Men were crudely blown in half, or neatly cleaved by fiery shards, or blasted backwards, or up, or died intact, or lived, though naked, or simply bled to death in static end-game stature. It was a good weapon. A cruel weapon. *He had left the computer on all night.*

"Fourth time this week," said Stevie, seating himself at his desk.

He waited for the dark faceless square to chameleon bloom; waited as the modem snapped invisible things to perfect place, then clicked the appropriate button.

> **Subject: Weaponry**
> **Date: 30 May 2001 7:12am**
> **From: silverspartan**
> **To: mimsypearl**
> An M-79 was a very large-bore, single-shot rifle which resembled a blunderbuss. It fired fist-sized 40mm shells in three flavors: buckshot, high explosive, and magnesium flares. In the jungle it was a good weapon. The North Vietnamese Army favored it over the M-16, which tended to jam and was hard to fix. Their standard weapon was much better. They were excellent soldiers too. I was lucky. Never wounded. My Lieutenant once shot a VC at close range. He caught a few dents. Nothing serious. Asked me to put him in for the Purple Heart. I said no. Well, time to make the donuts.

Her reply was instantaneous.

> **Subject: Purple Haze**
> **Date: 31 May 2001 7:21am**
> **From: mimsypearl**
> **To: silverspartan**
> What's with the numeric code? I didn't know you were in Sicily. Sounds like the M-79 was the best one, if you couldn't get the AK-47. See, I did my homework. Questions: Why didn't you want to recommend him for the purple heart? "Had shot a VC at close range." But in self defense, no? Are you free tomorrow night?

Stevie drummed the keyboard. "X X X X" Cross bones. Only the skull was missing. He pondered the startling sight of a brainless head which he once peered into. The soft irridescent lining suggested a fish pulled from water. Only the fish was a man and the man did not move and in strange repose seemed at rest.

Stevie lowered his head. Morning sunlight danced small circles across the bare white walls. Outside, cicadas trilled their high pitched tune. The effect was hypnotic. The fall into green time was sudden and brief.

("She's a fuckin dink," the machine gunner said, wiping blood from his boots. When Stevie knelt down the gunner rushed forward. The lieutenant pushed him aside. "No. We got enough today. She's POW. Go ahead, Doc." And Stevie pressed his canteen to enemy lips, suckling her back to life.)

Code. Numeric code. Beginning. Middle. End game. It was quiet now. Stevie looked about. He gathered his thoughts. Sacrifice. He must do that.

> **Subject: Lieutenant's Purple Heart Club Banned**
> **Date: 31 May 2001 7:49am**
> **From: silverspartan**
> **To: mimsypearl**
> Hey Cindy,
> Bet you're off to work. Story for another day that Purple Heart. Please understand.

Stevie stood up and walked to the kitchen. He began cursing. Louder, then louder still, unmercifully hurling abuse with each strident step. He would kick and kick the great white boxy beast. He would shatter all windows with his battering hands. He would crack brick walls by the force of his skull. He would scream and shout and blister with rage. Purple Heart? You want the Purple Heart? What about Corson? Shot through the lungs. And Bride. Six days and a wake up. What about the poor bastard you replaced? Sniped once in the hand, once in the head. I tried... I tried. Jesus fuckin Christ, sir. How many times do you need to hear it?

You did not get shot. You did not get hit. Stevie patched you up because you were good. You were very fuckin good. Nice shooting, sir. But you did not get shot. Not then. Not ever. And therefore, lieutenant, Stevie still loves you, he will always love you, he will always love all his men, but he no longer gives a flying fuck. Do you read me, sir? Do we have solid copy? All Stevie did was stay alive. That's all he did. Therefore, lieutenant, Stevie hereby refuses not to have a fuckin future. Or at least he'll fuckin try. With all due fuckin respect, sir, Stevie has got the right to kick the shit out of anybody or anything that keeps him from enjoying the sun, the trees, the snow, the sea, I mean, kick the motherfucker in the balls wants Stevie not to delight in birds or the touch of a woman.

Do you copy? I said do you fuckin copy? Who the fuck are you to get in the way of Stevie's life? You, sir, are but a deciduous memory much in need of sacerdotal dispensation. A ripe bead of shit in the rank outhouse of time. You cannot fucking sweat. You cannot fuckin laugh. Stevie's right to enjoy his life outranks you, lieutenant, no matter how much he fuckin loves you. No matter what you did for Stevie, he hereby declares, according to Robert's Rules, or the Geneva Convention, or the Rig fuckin Veda, or the Mafuckinbharata, Upanishads, Koran, the Holy fuckin Bible, the Lotus sutra, the Diamond sutra, the Rajna horse sacrifice, the Hymn of creation, Vishnu, Shiva, master's Basho, Chuan Tzu, Lao Tzu, the fuckin ardent Svetaketu, or He who in heaven is its highest fuckin surveyor. Oh with righteous saintly song and cloistered fuckin choir, my dear, dear, lieutenant, kindly shove that cursed star deep into the crimson folds of your royal fuckin ass. Yes, yes, Stevie will try hard, hard, to earn new ones. God will bestow them and Stevie will outrank every one else. Do you copy, sir? Stevie says do you fuckin copy? Good. That's real good. Cause Stevie's going AWOL from his memory's stockade and the enemy? The enemy is you, sir. And Stevie will give it his best shot, the motherfuckin best shot of all fuckin time, and you, sir, you will be wasted.

The words resounded a hundred times in the center of his soul.

When Stevie returned to his room he spoke to the empty monitor as if to a mentor, redeemer, best lover, friend.

"Damn you, Lieutenant," he said. "You son-of-a-bitch."

Then, with eyes half shut Stevie smiled a vague prelapsarian press-lipped grin. The kind which appear on smooth stone faced bodhisattvas lost in gold leaf bliss. The kind which grace those who by supreme martial will, stupendous luck or, paradoxically, dark Jobean nights, heart-sundering Jesuitical loss, arrive when sorrow and doubt—twin pillars of pilgrims misery—are sacrificed, surrendered, in a word—cast out. In the photography of his mind Stevie, who stood at convincing parade rest, recollected the event which had long steeped him in secret sorrow:

The casualty lay huddled inside the burning bunker. "C'mon," Stevie shouted, eyeing the stacked wood boxes packed with dull green hand grenades. "C'mon. This thing's gonna blow." But the wounded man could not hear him. Without thought Stevie crawled into the smoky pit and dragged him out. Months later someone said, "They got something for you, Doc. Better clean yourself up."

In fresh fatigues and shined boots Stevie had walked toward the company formation. Lieutenant Gill pointed him to place. Stevie looked expectantly at each man. In the relentless heat they stared straight back. A color guard, bright banners sagging, approached in strict, angular step. The lieutenant maintained silence. A major took hold of Stevie's fatigue shirt; a colonel read the citation. And they gave him the Silver Star.

"Fuck the computer," said Stevie, settling with pad and pencil on the bedroom floor. He missed the frictive feel of sharpened lead to white bleached paper. Taking his time, Stevie adjusted the triangulated pressure of thumb, middle and index finger around the easily snapped yellow implement.

It began simple enough, the polite use of discursive language, comfortable in length, moderate in detail, deft in plying crack bon mots and high-spirited phrases, the occasional four-letter word, the patois of war. Then came hurried diagrams depicting land and no-man's-land, the dread L-shaped ambush, the trip-wire detonated automatic ambush (composed of illegal Claymore mines staked at ground level, each sleek curved box contained two kilograms of C-4 plastic explosive and many hundred steel bearings), the slow accordion-rippling push of wide eyed men stagger-stepping forward on daily patrol. At length, he wrote heart-felt cameos of the men in his platoon, brief Aurelian meditations, cordial *pensees*. He did not mean to pour himself out on the page, attempting instead through varied and calibrated circumstance to convey the qualities of combat and what remained afterward. Stevie tried hard not to scold Cindy, nor berate, or patronize or impart canard, but state in practical detail the unerring chaos, the unpredictable beat, the cyclic consequences, the sorrow of war.

Of course Stevie wept. He heard and saw again the grand slam bang of corsairing artillery shells, the startling, high rising screams, the grotesque onion layers of organ and bone. He felt the lively kick and caterwaul above descending parachute flares; the *WRAP-WRAP-WRAP* of helicopters racing to attack. And always, always, the single word men used when calling for help: "Medic!" And Stevie would bind them and heal them, reveal impossible truths, provide comfort and care for those that lived. And, thus deceived, they took him and trusted him as one of their own. All this he wrote down, knowing full well Cindy could not know what she had not witnessed firsthand, and therefore, yes, Stevie would forgive her, just as he himself would never, ever forget.

Subject: Tickets
Date: 1 June 2001 7:23 am
From: mimsypearl
To: silverspartan
A friend gave me two tickets to "Miss Saigon." Are you free tomorrow night?

Stevie stared at the screen, then replied:

Subject: Just the Ticket
Date: 1 June 2001 7:30 am
From: silverspartan
To: mimsypearl
"Miss Saigon?" Sounds like fun.

Shirley Jolls and Walter Aponte

10 Kangaroo Court Martial

(March 10th, 1969). This is the strange case of George Daniels and William Harvey: two black Marines who got 6 and 10 years for opposing the Viet Nam War.

George Daniels and William Harvey are prisoners of the military dictatorship. Their "crime" is opposition to the war against Viet Nam, and the war against their own people, the men, women and children of Black America.

Corporal Harvey was railroaded through a brass-studded court-martial on November 27, 1967 and hit with the incredible sentence of six years imprisonment for allegedly making "disloyal statements."

A second panel of racist Marine Corps officers on December 7, 1967 slammed a ten year sentence on co-defendant Private Daniels for allegedly "advising, urging and attempting to cause insubordination, disloyalty and refusal of duty."

Neither Harvey nor Daniels was charged with committing any act—they were tried and imprisoned for their words alone!

The two black Marines are presently serving a total of sixteen years at hard labor in the Portsmouth, New Hampshire Brig.

Demonstrations called by the American Servicemen's Union and the Committee for GI Rights in New York, Seattle and Cleveland have broken the silence imposed for many months on this infamous frame-up. Their cases were recently heard by Military Review Boards, on appeal by the American Civil Liberties Union.

The case of Harvey and Daniels is among the most significant in the long list of political victims of the US military. From the Fort Hood Three, who refused to go to Viet Nam, Stolte and Amick who issued a call against the war, and the Fort Hood 43 who refused "riot control" duty—to the current courts-martial of the Presidio prisoners in California, no case more clearly shows the racist and totalitarian nature of the US military establishment.

The six and ten year sentences meted out to Harvey and Daniels for "disloyal words" are nearly unbelievable—until the circumstances are known. The following facts of the case are taken from the courts-martial records. They reveal the Brass' frame-up of the two men to be one more campaign in the war against Black America, and one more vicious attempt to make an example of anti-war soldiers—an example calculated to be so frightening that the Pentagon could begin to get the lid back on the simmering resistance in the Armed Forces.

William Harvey

Lance Corporal, USMC
Age 21
From Long Island City, NY
Enlisted June 1966
Previous convictions: none
Convicted 11/27/67 of "disloyal words"
Confined to Portsmouth, NH Disciplinary Barracks
For 6 years at hard labor.

(Photo shows trophy Harvey won as USMC welterweight boxing champion.)

George Daniels

Private First Class, USMC
Age 22
From St. Albans, NY
Enlisted August 1966
Previous convictions: none
Convicted 12/7/67 of "causing insubordination and disloyalty"
Confined to Portsmouth, NH Disciplinary Barracks
For 10 years at hard labor.

Black Marines Face Combat Duty in Viet Nam—or in Detroit

The time was July 1967, the place Camp Pendleton, California—Second Infantry Training Regiment of the US Marine Corps preparing thousands of young 'troopers' for combat duty in Viet Nam.

In the news: banner headlines on Detroit; casualty lists from Saigon.

These were the seeds of the Brass' rabid attack on Harvey and Daniels.

First there was a bull-session after noon chow among a group of black and white Marines. Then the talk took a turn that put the Brass uptight. Discussion turned to the war in Viet Nam and to the other war, the war against Black America.

The black Marines, particularly, were very much involved in the controversy. Within the past several weeks cops and National Guardsmen had been sent to put down heroic rebellions of black people in such far-flung cities as Cincinnati, Tampa, Buffalo, and—the biggest uprising up to that time—Detroit.

Any hour of the day these Marines could be ordered by the racist officers to shoot down black resistance fighters, just as they were soon to receive orders to level arms against another oppressed people, the Vietnamese.

Most of the Marines didn't like it, and they were intent on letting their objections be heard. Some apparently wanted out of the Marine Corps. Others were reported to have stated that under no condition would they bear arms against the black or Vietnamese people.

Request for "Mast" Termed Mutiny

During that day—July 27, 1967—a number of Afro-American Marines began to talk about 'requesting Mast,' a formal meeting with the commanding officer, to discuss the Viet Nam War and the 'riots.'

Theoretically, Mast is a procedure through which servicemen may register grievances, opinions, etc. with their superiors without fear or reprisal. This has been used by the military to let off steam from the rank and file. Usually the complaints are heard and that's the end of it. All power lies with the Brass, and things go on the way they were before.

But the act of black GIs gathering to let the officers know their feelings about the wars against Viet Nam and Black America was intolerable to the Brass. It was a threat to their supremacy, a challenge to the mindless discipline demanded by the 'elite.' So the Brass cracked down.

There was more on the officers' minds that morning than that suspicious bull-session, too—a fact which slipped out in testimony at Daniels' court-martial.

Major John Hilgers reported a separate incident at a class, during which two black Marines were ordered to perform double-time as punishment for some minor infraction of discipline. Instead of running 'on the double,' the men walked slowly off, and were joined by several other black Marines in a show of solidarity.

Another officer testified that the Second Infantry Training Regiment was a sort of reservoir of men who had been dropped from more desirable assignments, and were then being retrained for shipment to Viet Nam.

At morning formation on July 28, several black Marines, about 18 in number, were ordered to fall out and proceed to the Company Office. Their names were called from a list ferreted out by officers who had noticed the bull-session in the field the day before. The men were questioned one by one in what was supposedly a "screening" for the Mast, then threatened with mutiny charges.

In addition, many other men in the Company were interrogated by Naval Intelligence in a month-long campaign of intimidation. Some of them knew nothing about the bull-session until warned by ONI to "watch the people they went around with and just be careful of Daniels." To make doubly sure that the situation was back under control, the Brass singled out two black men, George Daniels and William Harvey, for the full force of military injustice.

Kangaroo Court-Martial

Captain Henry J. Trautwin, the officer who would have conducted the Mast, proffered charges against the two men. The Base Legal Office recommended General Courts-martial, and the trials were approved by Company Commander, Lt. Col. Neil Dimond.

Daniels and Harvey were subsequently arrested on August 17, 1967 and confined until the courts-martial four months later handed down the shattering sentences of six and ten years confinement at hard labor.

Originally both men were charged with promoting disloyalty. Harvey was charged with six specifications; that is, the Brass listed six Marines whom Harvey allegedly urged to refuse duty. Daniels' charges included sixteen such specifications. The two defendants were also accused of conspiring together to organize and conduct a "meeting" on July 27, 1967, at which Marines were advised to refuse duty in Viet Nam.

Even the hand-picked court-martial panel couldn't swallow the conspiracy charge, which was dropped at the very beginning of Harvey's trial. Nor had the four-month investigation dug up "proof" that Harvey had "promoted disloyalty."

Witness after witness described the gathering on July 27 as an informal one, a "bull-session." They indicated that the men had been listening to music and engaging in what could be described as a "barracks discussion."

Hellbent on getting some conviction, the court-martial found William Harvey guilty of "lesser charges" of disloyal statements, under the infamous Article 134 of the Universal Code of Military Justice (UCMJ). This so-called Devil's Article is a catch-all which sweepingly prohibits all "disloyal statements," that is, words which are "to the prejudice of good order and discipline in the Armed Forces," or of a "nature to bring discredit upon the Armed Forces."

For allegedly having stated "the black man should not go to Viet Nam and fight the white man's war," Harvey was sentenced to reduction to the lowest rank, forfeiture of all pay, dishonorable discharge and the maximum of six years in military prison.

The second panel dropped the conspiracy charge against Daniels also—reluctantly deciding that it takes two to conspire. But this time the kangaroo court-martial stuck to the more serious charge and, building on Harvey's conviction, railroaded George Daniels under Section 2387, a Smith Act provision of the US Criminal Code. This includes: "Making statements with intent to impair or interfere with the discipline, morale or fulfillment of duty by a member of the Armed Forces."

For allegedly maintaining that "the black man should not fight in Viet Nam because he would have to come back and fight the white man in the United States," Daniels received the maximum sentence of reduction to the lowest rank, forfeiture of all pay, dishonorable discharge and ten years in military prison.

Daniels was the prime victim because the Brass had portrayed him as a ringleader, and claimed that he had been advocating, "impairment of discipline" over a period of months, from his Basic Training at Cherry Point, NC through the incidents of July 1967.

Captain Henry J. Trautwein stated that Daniels had previously discussed with him the possibility of a change of MOS (military occupational specialty) for religious reasons. The effect of this standard military procedure was reported by Trautwein's superior, Major John Hilgers who testified that he was therefore aware that Daniels was a Muslim, and he had "just told Captain Trautwein to keep an eye on him and let me know, one, if he was going to assume a CO status; two, if he was influencing the morale or discipline of the Command, because I believe at the time Captain Trautwein said that he had seen them or seen Daniels talking to some other Marine."

News of Legal Lynching Breaks through Marine Corps Cover-Up

During the months between the July incident and the convictions in late November and early December, the Brass managed to keep their preparations for the courts-martial secret—and the establishment press went along with the censorship. So extensive was this cover-up that most people in the anti-war movement did not even hear of the frame-up until long after the trials.

But news of such unspeakable injustice gets through even prison walls and eventually the American Servicemen's Union learned of the case and broke the story in the June 11, 1968 issue of its newspaper, *The Bond*. At the same time Melvin L. Wulf of the American Civil Liberties Union, with Edward F. Sherman of the Harvard Law School and Conrad Lynn, began preparing appeal briefs at the long-silenced request of the defendants.

Any soldier can testify that the UCMJ offers no protection against the arbitrary rule of the officer caste. And when the Code gets in the Brass' way, even the thin veil of it, 'justice' is torn to shreds—as in the implacable drive to get Harvey and Daniels.

The denial of even the most rudimentary rights supposedly guaranteed by the UCMJ is impressively detailed in the UCLA appeal briefs to the Military Review board as follows. Denial of free speech. Bias by the presiding officer, constituting denial of a fair and impartial trial. Denial of chosen counsel. Admittance of erroneous confessions. Denial of confrontation of witnesses, amounting to suppression of evidence. Cruel and unusual punishment.

Pentagon Calls It a "Wildcat Strike!"

On March 6, 1969, two Navy Boards of Review at the Washington, DC Navy Yard heard the appeals. Harvey and Daniels were represented by Edward Sherman, acting for the ACLU. The *New York Times* of the following day reported the appeals as "a test of the military's power to punish enlisted men who dissent against the Viet Nam War."

As of this writing the Review Boards have given no indication regarding their decisions, nor suggested when the judgments might be handed down from the Pentagon.

Captain Lester G. Fant 3d, arguing the case for the Marine Corps, made crystal clear the real nature and the origin of the frame-up of George Daniels and William Harvey. This Pentagon lawyer described the situation at Camp Pendleton in July 1967 as "extraordinarily dangerous" and compared it to a "wildcat strike!"

The Brass was obviously scared by the events of opposition which bubbled up in those summer days of 1967. They lashed out viciously to put down any manifestation of anti-war sentiment and, particularly, any support for the black liberation movement.

"An example to other Marines"

The prosecutor in the Harvey court-martial, Captain Paul R. Constantino, stated the officers' intentions very openly in his recommendation for the maximum sentence:

> "We are asking you to punish William Harvey so that others may know that conditions such as this cannot and will not be tolerated in the Marine Corps or in the military service... the accused stands as an example and the government submits to the court that the sentence which the court will impose on the accused will also serve as an example to the other Marines..."

Captain John C. Stein, for the prosecution team in Daniels' trial ended his request for conviction by reminding the panel that one witness "testified that George Daniels said to him that he would rather go to jail than fight for his country. The government respectfully urges that you grant George Daniels' request."

Numerous details of the Brass' persecution of Harvey and Daniels have come to light. The two black Marines were "advised" not to get civilian attorneys, so that the case could be "quietly" handled by military defense lawyers from the Judge Advocate General's office. The Brass tried to make it all appear like a sort of family affair—but were actually conducting a secret trial, which is totally illegal and unconstitutional.

ONI agents went through the whole Company to gather the prosecution witnesses. These flunkies also maneuvered Harvey and Daniels into making "statements" without the advice of personal counsel. The interrogators dictated "confessions" and submitted these constructed documents to the courts-martial as "evidence."

The JAG defense lawyers, Captain Richard J. Riordan and 2nd Lt. Thomas Schwindt, had little time to speak to Marines who were to take the stand at the order of the Marine Corps. In fact, some of these men had been returned from duty in Viet Nam just as the trials began. The Law Officer at Harvey's trial actually apologized to the panel of Brass for presenting these witnesses in their battle fatigues. Several men were given leave immediately after questioning by ONI, and were never subsequently available for examination by Defense Counsel.

On the recommendations of Brass in the Base Legal Office, Harvey and Daniels were court-martialled separately, the better to play one case off against the other. The defense lawyers, after originally working on the cases jointly, had little opportunity even to consult each other once the trials began. The lawyer assigned to Harvey was advocating his first case in court, and stated that he felt himself too inexperienced for such a serious case.

Racist Brass Fear Black Liberation Movement

Both Harvey and Daniels are followers of the Nation of Islam, and every minute of their trials shows the racist reaction of the white officers to the accused's belief in self-determination for black people.

Racism shows in little as well as important ways. The court stenographers often recorded black witnesses as saying "he axed me," or "I axed him."

More significantly, a member of the panel in Daniels' trial, Lt. Samuel M. Gordan, stated under Defense questioning as to his attitude about nationalism:

> "...if I knew in advance that (a man assigned to my command) was a Black Muslim and advertising this fact, this would to my mind mean trouble and I could see—I could foresee problems..."

Captain Benjamin H. Berry, presiding as Law Officer, became so enraged by one witness' statements on the status of black people in the United States that he called for an out-of-court hearing (similar to a session in a judge's Chambers) to release his frustration at not being able to step down from the bench to challenge the black man's credibility. Adding to the illegal advocacy of the prosecution case, Berry tered out this racist formula:

> "...I must profess I am profoundly shocked. Profoundly shocked. I was raised with Negroes. I have know[n] Negroes all my life. I have a very high respect for Negroes and I do not believe one-tenth of what I read in that—and we speak of 'Negro ghettos' and I have been in the Negro section of town many times, and I don't believe one-tenth of that."

The picture of Captain Berry can be rounded out by his rejection of Defense Counsel's motion to dismiss the case against Daniels on the Constitutional grounds of free speech and freedom of assembly:

> "A very strict and narrow construction of the First Amendment would certainly support the argument that you have made, but... (it) recalled to my mind the statement—and I don't recollect right now who it was that made it, but—'My country, right or wrong, is still my country' and I think that as a matter of Constitutional law that pretty well wraps up the expression of what the situation is, and we do not have the right, so long as we are citizens of this country to attempt to impair this country."

From mid-August until the courts-martial opened, Harvey and Daniels were isolated from their fellow Marines and from any possible support. Daniels spent all but about three weeks in a "segregation cell"—solitary confinement—admittedly because of his views as a Muslim.

Taken all together, the circumstances of Harvey and Daniels' frame-up show one of the most flagrant cases of kangaroo justice in the history of the US Marine Corps; the kind of occurrence which shows the US Military to be anything but the guardian of "American democracy" its officers and the big business politicians profess it to be.

Anti-War Soldiers Need Organized Support

The anti-war movement has only recently become aware of the strong resistance within the Armed Forces by GIs against the war, the Brass, and the fascistic military establishment. Such resistance began individually, but has become more organized, with increasing militancy and assertiveness on the part of the soldiers. At the same time the frightened Brass has been reacting with increasing viciousness against the rebellious soldiers.

The pioneers of resistance within the Armed Forces, Johnson, Samas and Mora of the valiant Fort Hood Three, were given from three to four years for refusing to go to Viet Nam. Harvey and Daniels received six and ten years for nothing more than speaking out against the war.

Countless other GIs have been court-martialed, fined, restricted, investigated and imprisoned for their opposition to the tyranny of the Brass.

More recently the Pentagon committed another outrage against all GIs; at the courts-martial of the Presidio stockade prisoners for their protest against the murder of a fellow prisoner at the hands of an MP, as well as against the inhuman conditions in the stockade. The first three of these prisoners got sentences ranging from thirteen to sixteen years.

In several cases, on the other hand, GIs have won partial victories because of publicity obtained for their cases, and because of the mobilization of civilian support by groups such as the Committee for GI Rights. Intervention by the American Servicemen's Union has been particularly helpful—as in the trials of the 43 black GIs at Fort Hood in late 1968. These soldiers made it known that they would refuse duty in the suppression of any black rebellion or anti-war activity during the 1968 Democratic Convention in Chicago. The ASU coordinated legal defense and with a delegation from the Committee for GI Rights, helped to focus national attention on the trials. Consequently, the Brass had to back off a long way and give relatively mild punishment.

Put the Brass on Trial!

The Brass' frame-up of Harvey and Daniels came easier because these men were isolated not only from the other Marines in their Company, but from any civilian support they may have wanted. It is too late to intervene against the Pentagon's offensive of July 1967, but it remains for the anti-war movement to make their case known nationwide and to raise a cry for their release which will penetrate the walls of the Portsmouth Brig.

The case of George Daniels and William Harvey should justly end in putting the Brass on trial and handing down approximate retribution for their crimes against these two black Marines and every other brig and stockade prisoner.

* * *

The Committee for GI Rights supports the American Servicemen's Union, the foremost organization of soldiers in the US Armed Forces. The ASU has grown enormously since its founding in December, 1967, and now has members at all major military bases in the US and around the world.

UNION DEMANDS

- An end to saluting and sir-ring of officers—let's get off our knees.
- Election of officers by vote of the men.
- Racial equality.
- Rank and filers control of court-martial boards.
- Federal minimum wage.
- The right of free political association.
- The right of collective bargaining.
- The right to disobey illegal orders—like orders to go and fight in an illegal war in Viet Nam.

Staff: Pvt. Andy Stapp (ret.), PFC F.O. Richardson (ret.), PFC Bill Smith (ret.), Sp/4 Dick Wheaton (ret.) and Sp/5 Bob LeMay (ret.)

AN APPEAL FROM THE BRIG:

"...now it's your turn."

Note that the last time we dealt with these beasts, we asked that I be released. This time we demand.

This may sound radical to you but what was done to us was radical. Two men sentenced to six and ten years for dissenting against the war? The reason is because we are black, intelligent, and refuse to be pushed. Niggers just ain't supposed to act like that! While I was brainwashed into believing that the cause for going overseas was a just cause, I did show that I would put on a uniform and fight if necessary to protect people like you. Now that we are hip to what's really happening, it's the people's turn to protect me. Only they don't have to pick up rifles, just pens. Hang petitions in the Candy Store, Herman's, the Center, and every other place you can think of because now it's your turn.

Note: (Portions of a letter from George Daniels to a friend in his hometown.)

The American Servicemen's Union (ASU) was formed in 1968 by active-duty GIs who opposed the Viet Nam War and oppression within the military. At its height it had 160 chapters on bases in the U.S. and overseas on 50 U.S. Navy ships. In 1971, its newspaper *The Bond* was mailed to 20,000 service people and reached thousands more as it was passed hand to hand. Its programmatic demands included the election of officers by the ranks; no use of troops against strikers, anti-war demonstrators, or the oppressed communities; an end to racism and sexism in the military and the right to collective bargaining. The ASU was the subject of an *Esquire* magazine article in August 1968 entitled "The Plot to Unionize the Army."

Postscript (September 23rd, 1969)

"Pvt. Daniels had been convicted two years ago of counseling insubordination and disloyalty with intent to interfere with loyalty, morale, and discipline of members of the armed forces. Cpt. Harvey was convicted at the same time of making disloyal statements. Daniels was sentenced to 10 years imprisonment and Harvey to 6 years. Their sentences were reduced to 4 years and 3 years, respectively early in the summer by a Navy Board of Review. What is most astounding, of course, is that so elementary an aspect of civil liberties such as the right to be free during appeal procedures has to be fought for. Beyond that, as ACLU Legal Director Melvin Wult said, 'They should never have been in prison at all because their convictions are in our opinion unconstitutional. They were not convicted of doing anything except expressing their opposition to the war in Vietnam and their support of the struggle for freedom for blacks at home. Their prosecution and conviction was a flagrant violation by the Marine Corps of protected first amendment rights.'

If freedom of speech has any meaning at all then it means freedom for the most controversial of ideas. To those who would argue that there should be no freedom of speech in the military we might remind them of the terrible deeds that were justified in the German Army during World War II through just such a conception of the soldier as uncritical order obeying robot."

Arthur E. Hippler
President Alaska Civil Liberties Union

11 Poetry

Dayl Wise

Found Photograph

Black and white photograph,
Dad in foreground,
Army dress uniform,
a pose I'm familiar with,
hands at side, slightly forward,
proud pose, shoulders back.
A found photograph
from your footlocker
loose among others,
taken in France many years ago.
The part of you I don't know.

On a street, maybe Paris,
a theater in the background,
people, well dressed, walking by.

Some appear to enter.
A soldier, near theater door
stares up street at someone or something.
A woman to your left,
clutching a pocketbook, hurries past,
not aware her image is before me.
It's daytime.
Did you go to the matinee
with your friend?

Twenty-eight years after your death,
who took this picture?
A soldier from your unit?
A grease monkey like you,
Midwesterner, tall, blond?
A French woman
Petite, red lipstick,
Silk stockings,
the ones with dark seams
running up the back?

Dayl Wise

Alan Farrell

Fighting Position

Sunshafts settle through the thick jungle canopy
Illumine sporadically the level verge of a deepsetstream
Quilt of sunsquares on the jungle floor where men have stood before us
Now gone Christknowswhere
Batallion basecamp says the aerial overlay
But down here it looks as if a few miserable dinks could squat
A few miserable days
Then move
On

These things are always the same
Cut into ridgelines hacked into hilltops sunk along brooksides
A living place wrenched from the hostile vegetation
Semicircles of holes where a man might hide
Hunkered down in the darkness with his thoughts
From whatever horror the embrace of dirt could possibly console
A few miserable minutes
Then move
On

There's a regulation field latrine regulation downstream
Regulation cookfirepits buried into the slope and openvented to hide smoke regulation
And a regulation classroom area for regulation
Indoctrination and the updating of political propositions
Rough benches seats regulation even frames for regulation blackboards
Ideas can die so suddenly in the jungle or live just
A few miserable days
Then move
On

They were here ate slept hunched drilled and most
Of all hacked out these holes no not just holes
Says the Captain Fighting Positions a hole is what a grunt
Chops in the fetid rot after humping all day caved in sides

Dirt slung hell to breakfast utilitarian hasty hole
But these are still perfect after the diggers have dwelt
A few miserable months
Then move
On

Absolutely geometrical square-sided plumb level
Sides raked down flawless and almost polished
Floor of the position we must call it position now
Flat and true-cornered drained built to endure to gouge
Human will into a recalcitrant jungle who will make
Her half hearted effort at eroding them washing them out growing them over
A few miserable weeks
Then move
On

Fighting positions the Captain says these are professionals
Not halfass stumblers like us they live here we visit
And in this slime and muck disease and heat under this eternal green shroud
Wracked with dysentery malaria dengue Christknowswhat not
To speak of what gnaws a man's soul out here
They carved these monuments to their own feverish glory to endure in time
A few miserable moments
Then move
On

Alan Farrell

The Tom

You'd be disappointed if you ever saw a photo and even more if you had to drag your tired
Ass and your refrigerator plus whatever's in the trunk of your see-dan right now forty kilo
Meters up and down the tiers of a football stadium in the rain with a mouthful of cigarette ash to
Get there nothing but a dirt lane the Ho Chi Minh Trail
I've pissed on it thank you

Tom's a road in radio code this one's the Ho Chi Minh
Humpin' rucks or drivin' trucks the traffic's never thin
Fin' it mine it map align it
Site it fight it Arc Light it
But don't ever never ever be such a dumb sonuvabitch as to try an' walk it…

Tom has legs each with a commander quadrant cohort its own security force
Cooks roadgangs mechanics guides Christknowswhatall
But you set a soiled *tou bi* foot on that thing dumb Gringo
And you wake 'em all up tha's the fac', Jack
And they'll be after you swarm of wasps chase you back into the jungle you stumbled out of

Tom's a road in radio code this one's the Ho Chi Minh
Humpin' rucks or drivin' trucks the traffic's never thin
Fin' it mine it map align it
Site it fight it Arc Light it
But don't ever never ever be such a dumb sonuvabitch as to try an' walk it…

They crank those ZILs till they can't no more then feed the parts into another carcass
Nothing but a '48 Chevy so far as we can tell
Stake and platform double rear wheels whiny old gears
Hear 'em growlingprowling moaninggroaning painingstraining up the grade

Doubleclutch downshift then the next one count make lines and bars my soggynotepad

Tom's a road in radio code this one's the Ho Chi Minh
Humpin' rucks or drivin' trucks the traffic's never thin
Fin' it mine it map align it
Site it fight it Arc Light it
But don't ever never ever be such a dumb sonuvabitch as to try an' walk it...

They park the trucks daytime in truck ports dugbyhanddug into the mountainside
Play cards grabass chase the *congai* write up their paperwork pull maintenance
Then comes dark they roll
Christknowswhere upthendown and backagain no lights by braille
Endless antlike ferrying of those big cake crumbs

Tom's a road in radio code this one's the Ho Chi Minh
Humpin' rucks or drivin' trucks the traffic's never thin
Fin' it mine it map align it
Site it fight it Arc Light it
But don't ever never ever be such a dumb sonuvabitch as to try an' walk it...

We sit and watch 'em like kids watching ants *kiem cang* they say "strong as an ant"
Sturdy little buggers freighting those enormous loads of stuff we've spilt or wouldn't touch
No discernible purpose pain hope remorse passion
Just pack that stuff from where there's no evident reason to where there's nothing more
And backagain

Tom's a road in radio code this one's the Ho Chi Minh
Humpin' rucks or drivin' trucks the traffic's never thin
Fin' it mine it map align it
Site it fight it Arc Light it
But don't ever never ever be such a dumb sonuvabitch as to try an' walk it...

We lay out in the dark jungle count 'em record 'em transmit 'em
Jeeezus that one's fulla guys howling do they spot me
I see them boiling off that truck shouldertoshoulder sweeping this roadside
Flush me like a rabbit I can already
Feel my lungs ache scuttling up that hill rucksack radio weapon chow ammo smoke flares Jeezus

Tom's a road in radio code this one's the Ho Chi Minh
Humpin' rucks or drivin' trucks the traffic's never thin
Fin' it mine it map align it
Site it fight it Arc Light it
But don't ever never ever be such a dumb sonuvabitch as to try an' walk it…

But they're not shouting There's a roundeye let's catch 'im and cornhole 'im
Instead it's some kinda patriot anthem
Bullshit song hymn to *camaraderaderaderie* groupfuck solidararararity
Ten thousand years of life to Uncle Ho glory to the People or
I'd rather ride this bitch than walkalkalk

Tom's a road in radio code this one's the Ho Chi Minh
Humpin' rucks or drivin' trucks the traffic's never thin
Fin' it mine it map align it
Site it fight it Arc Light it
But don't ever never ever be such a dumb sonuvabitch as to try an' walk it…

Once I lose the toss and have to sneak down there right out onto that planed laterite
Step in a footdeep ditch that road is ditched I'm here to say
Slam facedown with all my gear straps buckles pouches grenades mines ammo canteens KA-BAR
Strobe compass cleaningrod P(*roject*) I(*ndigenous*) R(*ation*)s panel fuck
With a clatter like the Devil dropped his mess kit somehow nobody hears

Tom's a road in radio code this one's the Ho Chi Minh
Humpin' rucks or drivin' trucks the traffic's never thin
Fin' it mine it map align it
Site it fight it Arc Light it
But don't ever never ever be such a dumb sonuvabitch as to try an' walk it...

Sweatingyeahsweating in the cold night air
Two 'yards security up and down trail I scratch a hole two three and do the deed
Ih-hinnnnnnnnnnnnnnfinite caution my nowbananafingers can't holdmoldfold
Arming pin won't come fuckshitfuck loose gently really sweating now yank that thing
Dirt back scatterlevelsmooth my tracks sign it like a Picasso goddam moon

Tom's a road in radio code this one's the Ho Chi Minh
Humpin' rucks or drivin' trucks the traffic's never thin
Fin' it mine it map align it
Site it fight it Arc Lightit
But don't ever never ever be such a dumb sonuvabitch as to try an' walk it...

Now it seems to me like I've done a professional
Job but you can probably see that bitch a mile off anyhow comes two ay emm
And the nightly caravan rumbles up the valley grindingwindingbinding
Accordion convoy will he find my handywork will he flush me after
Scared skinny but curious enough to die to see it

Tom's a road in radio code this one's the Ho Chi Minh
Humpin' rucks or drivin' trucks the traffic's never thin
Fin' it mine it map align it
Site it fight it Arc Light it
But don't ever never ever be such a dumb sonuvabitch as to try an' walk it...

I'm waiting for Eniwetok it's instead a pathetic
Ba-woom muffled by the dirt and the steel but it shears the spindle
Blows that wheel treehigh launches rim and tire off into the jungle
Thrashingcrashingsmashing through the underbrush
Musta blinked didn't even see the flash

Tom's a road in radio code this one's the Ho Chi Minh
Humpin' rucks or drivin' trucks the traffic's never thin
Fin' it mine it map align it
Site it fight it Arc Light it
But don't ever never ever be such a dumb sonuvabitch as to try an' walk it...

Now they're out with flashlights jabbering in that heathen *patois* of theirs
I beat it back up the next ridge tell the Captain I got one
Blundering into trees hung up on vines in the dark see with your feet see *this* you fuck
Gasp my way up to the R(*endezvous*) O(*ver*) N(*ight*) soaked in sweat lie back savor my triumph
In the stillness moon glowers at me stillness what

Tom's a road in radio code this one's the Ho Chi Minh
Humpin' rucks or drivin' trucks the traffic's never thin
Fin' it mine it map align it
Site it fight it Arc Light it
But don't ever never ever be such a dumb sonuvabitch as to try an' walk it...

Grumble of motors shriek of gears they're moving again how
The time it takes me to bull my way fivehundred meters of blacknightblack jungle
They're back on their way
The time it'd take me to go up and fish out another mine and blunder back down
They're gone and don't even bother to chase me

Tom's a road in radio code this one's the Ho Chi Minh
Humpin' rucks or drivin' trucks the traffic's never thin
Fin' it mine it map align it

Site it fight it Arc Light it
But don't ever never ever be such a dumb sonuvabitch as to try an' walk it...

They've chained the dead ox to his buddy's rear bumper and wound off
I'm beat to hell but I crawl back down to exactly justexactlyjust where I sank that mine
Silence wail of gears receding feebly into distance silence truck gone hole gone for Chrissake they even filled in my hole I sweep a hand across the dewy earth
One lousy lockwasher

Tom's a road in radio code this one's the Ho Chi Minh
Humpin' rucks or drivin' trucks the traffic's never thin
Fin' it mine it map align it
Site it fight it Arc Light it
But don't ever never ever be such a dumb sonuvabitch as to try an' walk it...

And if they don't chase me that night
It's only cause wasn't their job to chase us next morning firstlight
Here comes fifty motivated sonuvabitches whose job it *is* to chase us run us three days
Signal shots sounds like right the hell over the ridgeline hat up again three days
Before we can even dare stop to hunt for an LZ

Tom's a road in radio code this one's the Ho Chi Minh
Humpin' rucks or drivin' trucks the traffic's never thin
Fin' it mine it map align it
Site it fight it Arc Light it
But don't ever never ever be such a dumb sonuvabitch as to try an' walk it...

Next time Captain says we'll call in a fuckin' road cut from three clicks off
But F(*orward*) O(*perational*) B(*ase*) tells him You *will* mine that bitch so Captain wakes me up at oh

Two hundred Gimme the radio Sun King Sun King Tallow Pulley over I'm on the Tom over he whispers

Doing the deed at this time over he whispers uh-hunh puff deed uh-hunh whuff d-d-d-d-d-done over

Panting eversoslightly doan wanna oversell it into the handset nice touch goes back to sleep

Tom's a road in radio code this one's the Ho Chi Minh
Humpin' rucks or drivin' trucks the traffic's never thin
Fin' it mine it map align it
Site it fight it Arc Light it
But don't ever never ever be such a dumb sonuvabitch as to try an' walk it…

So it goes on the Tom hunnerd fifty three I count ninety-six I count eighty one I count vehicles

One morning first light they're hustling a last run down the misty track twenny three I count

I'm under a poncho scratching lines and bars my soggynotepad twenny four I count then spot 'im

Viet trail officer through the roadside leavesbriarsvines *his* soggynotepad scratching *his* lines and bars…Jeeezus wept

Tom's a road in radio code this one's the Ho Chi Minh
Humpin' rucks or drivin' trucks the traffic's never thin
Fin' it mine it map align it
Site it fight it Arc Light it
But don't ever never ever be such a dumb sonuvabitch as to try an' walk it…

Ho Chi Minh Trail: named after Ho Chi Minh, leader of the revolution It was a vast NVA and VC supply route
ZILs: Russian all purpose trucks used in Vietnam
Congais: Vietnamese girls
Eniwetok: The Battle of Eniwetok was during the Pacific campaign of World War II

Rich Raitano

12 Absent of Grace and Mercy

USS Gordon circa mid-1960s (courtesy: Naval Historical Center)

On December 19th, 1967, four days after my twenty-third birthday, the USS Gen. W. H. Gordon slipped slowly and gently into Qui Nhon Bay, Republic of South Viet Nam. I was a medic with HHC (Headquarters and Headquarters Company) / 4th Battalion / 3rd Infantry Regiment (The Old Guard) / 11th Light Infantry Brigade.

In early March, 1968, after spending time on LZ Sue with Bravo Company, and stays at the aid stations on Hill 54 and LZ Bronco, I was assigned to 2nd Surgical Hospital in Chu Lai as Casualty Reporter / Hospital Liaison for our battalion and Task Force Barker. My primary duties were to assess, evaluate and interview our unit wounded when they arrived from the battlefield, and report to Battalion S-2.

I made daily visits to the wards, spending time talking with each man, bringing Red Cross supplied sundries or requested materials from the PX, and when called to do so, tour with unit officers who came to visit with their wounded troops.

The most difficult function of my assignment were the visits to GR (Graves Registration) to identify, assess, evaluate, and confirm cause of death. Most of these men were known to me from the early days of our training at Schofield Barracks, Hawaii. Many were friends. All were brothers.

An insufferable despair hung heavy along the murky waters of Acheron. Thick, black clouds tumbled and swirled with frenzied rage in a blood red sky.

Dark, unearthly shadows drifted uneasily above the charred and ashen landscape. It was an eternally damned place, chosen to serve as an un-holy tabernacle for mayhem and carnage; for fear and endless sorrow. No God or gods dare walk there; it was absent of grace and mercy.

The dog tired and sweat drenched platoon stumbled into the clearing. web-gear and tired asses hit the ground. Smokes were lit. Small talk and muffled laughter rolled uneasily in the sticky May night.

It was good to stop, to finally end their nomadic trek through jungle brush, and rice paddy muck in search of an elusive enemy. One by one each man settled in for the night.

All was not well.

As quick as a raging torrent and roaring thunder comes in an unexpected storm, the jungle erupted into a deadly and frantic fury. Hot, angry projectiles stampeded through the musty air, cutting a path of instant death. Shouts and screams filled the windless night. Then all was as swiftly still and silent.

The foul stench of death hung heavily around them, clinging to their clothes, filling their lungs. The deadly incense of cordite pierced the air in the retreating twilight.

A tattered paperback lay on the grassy rise; an outstretched hand gripped the curled and sweat stained pages. Bloodied fingers clawed in vain at the soft earth in a hopeless attempt to escape the coming tempest.

The weary, faltering rhythm of his fading heart summoned the demons to gather in ghoulish anticipation; waiting patiently for the moment when all is forever lost and the profane feast that would soon begin. The vital glow of his life grew pale and dim. One last image lay unseen in empty cold eyes, one final thought fell short of lasting memory. And in the ominous silence between now and never, the desperate struggle for life and death began.

His life's blood ran warm through the hands of those who worked in vain to save him. They could not comprehend that he was already gone; the life they knew to be his had been torn from this world and flung carelessly into another.

Only the dead and dying heard the pitiless triumphant mockery as it moved in the ground beneath them...

May 8, 1968

My thoughts were wildly conflicted as I sprinted through the maze of screened wooden hooches of 2nd Surgical Hospital in Chu Lai. Delta Company had made contact and the wounded and dead were on the way. I waited uneasily at the pad for dust-off to arrive. My heart pounded in my ears and my lungs sucked in the heavy night air.

One of our medics was a casualty. Andy, Fred, and Leroy were medics with Delta Company. In the distant darkness the familiar cadence of blades slicing into the dank air worked its way into my anxieties. I watched with pained anguish as dust-off approached, touched down, and the wounded were off-loaded and rushed into the ER.

Gathering myself, I took a deep breath and followed them. The smell of blood and torn flesh filled the room. Doctors, nurses, and hospital medics went from litter to litter treating first those with the best chance of survival.

I slowly made my way to each litter, taking names and assessing wounds while searching for the medic. He was not among them. One of the wounded told me that "doc was hit" but could tell me nothing more.

I rejected the thought of where he could be and struggled with the persistent gnawing truth as I made my way out of the ER and trotted down the darkened road to Graves Registration (GR). I had done this so many times before and I knew he was there, but I would not say it; I would not dare think it.

The fridge room was dimly lit and cool. I had come to appreciate this room and the macabre opportunity it offered for escape from the hot and oppressive air outside its walls. On most occasions, the attendant would pull cool beers from an empty drawer while I examined the bodies of fallen comrades. With emotions shut down it had become nothing more than a daily routine: assess and evaluate the dead and wounded, drink a beer and exchange smalltalk. Such is the stolid necessity that separates the living from the dead.

GR was nothing more than a grim crypt with a never-ending supply of dead. Time and countless visits had kindly dulled my senses. But that night, May 8th, the room would not willingly receive me. Struggling against my desire to turn and walk away, I made my way to the desk and asked about the recent delivery. The attendant led me to a drawer, pulled it open and unzipped the body bag.

It was Fred.

I stepped back as the hopelessness of his death struck me. The room went silent, and my head filled with an incredulous roar as the sinister, cold specter of death rushed past me once again; looked me in the eyes and moved on.

"GSW to the back of the head," the attendant reported with a casual indifference as he turned and went about his business; his own senses numbed long ago.

A tight, knotted pressure began building in my chest and my head ached as I looked on the lifeless body of my friend. His face was unshaven and sweat streaked...and warm still to the touch. I gently lifted his head and located the entry wound. No exit. I wept silently for my friend; his life now gone. My tears fell on his body.

I was just two months into my duties as a Casualty Reporter and I had seen much death and mayhem already, and much more would follow before my tour was over, but this one was personal and filled with cruel irony.

In mid-January 1968, while pulling guard on LZ Sue, the word had come to us that another friend, Dave, had been killed. It was a friendly fire incident. As the platoon was moving through rice paddies, Dave reached up and grabbed the barrel of Fred's M-16 to pull himself up. A shot rang out and a round entered Dave's chest under his arm. In a matter of seconds he was dead.

Fred was devastated and noticeably changed when I saw him again sometime later. He was more subdued; quiet. The weight of that death hung heavy and hard on his spirit.

And now he was dead.

I turned and walked into the humid oppressive air. My body shook with anger and grief while the past, present and future collided in my head. I was physically and mentally exhausted from the goddamned daily bloody mayhem of torn and shattered bodies and watching men die. I had had enough.

I screamed at God that night as I made my way up the road. I could no longer contain my rage or my tears. I wanted the forces of Heaven to explain this to me.

The urgent cacophony of busy choppers was the only reply I heard that night as I made my way back to the ER under a star filled sky. God was silent...and Heaven was far from near.

~~~

The aged USS Gordon cut smoothly through the blue-gray ocean, slowly rising and falling, sending a glittering salty mist over the bow in the early morning sun. We gathered to watch in fascination as a school of porpoise frolicked alongside; rising and plunging, leading the way.

Later that evening as the sun was setting; Fred, Jim, Andy, Lee, and I sat on the steel deck talking in low hushed tones discussing our impending fate. We were in a reflective and somber mood that December night as we steamed towards Viet Nam. Up to that time we had managed to avoid any discussion of our private thoughts and fears. We laughed and joked and ran about the ship as if on a cruise, or another training exercise. But it could be stilled no longer.

The disquieting reality of what lay ahead of us had finally surfaced and demanded that we acknowledge its presence. From that sullen moment forward we saw each day as if it were the last, and one another as if for the last time. That sense of powerless never left us. It was a simple fact; one year from that moment it was a certainty that one or more of us would be dead. It was an un-welcomed and forbidding thought.

Somewhere on deck, accompanied by several low voices, a guitarist strummed softly amidst the many muffled conversations around us. The whole ship seemed to have been gripped by the same haunting uneasiness that night.

The sun now long set, we sat silent, lost in our private thoughts. Fred quietly disturbed the silence with what now seems to have been a prescient thought. It has remained with me through all these years...

"If I die..." he softly announced, "I want to die for *a cause*, not just *be-cause*."

Just twenty-five days from his twenty-first birthday, Fred failed to get his wish.

It was silent and still. The shadows grew restless; aroused with vile expectation and hungry for the souls delivered to them in this bitter place.

A shrill and demonic wailing echoed from the depths of the blackness. The time had come.

Death rose from the putrid depths and stood triumphantly above the tragedy before him. And with a cool indifference, he raised his staff to signal the gruesome feast to begin.

December 5, 1967

We watched in apprehensive silence as the glittering lights of Waikiki faded slowly into the inky black South Pacific night. It was December 5th, 1967, and our time in the Hawaiian paradise had come to its end. Months of training had shaped us, the 11th Light Infantry Brigade, into the *Jungle Warriors*. We were called to action by General Westmoreland who believed we were ready to battle the communist enemy on the other side of the globe.

Huddled aft on the USS Gordon, we strained to catch the last fading glimpses of the world we were leaving: warm sandy beaches, tanned and bikinied beauties, and most of all...our youth.

The shoreline shimmered softly like a strand of diamonds resting on the obsidian night as we sailed away to war. It flickered as if to say *aloha*...and then was gone.

The mood on ship was pensive and solemn as we stared into an empty and dark ocean. Quiet and reserved conversations could be heard as the gray merchant ship cut its way through the water. We knew that within this coming year many of us would be killed. Who amongst us would not return?

The answer was out there yet...somewhere beyond the horizon...waiting for us.

LZ Carentan (December 1967)

The Huey shook as the turbine whined and reached for peak power. The giant rotor blades whistled and accelerated smoothly above us, cutting into the hot air, sending a swirling, reddish dust-cloud billowing in all directions. The chopper shivered slightly with anticipation, and then at the pilot's command, we rose gracefully and began our journey to LZ Sue. It was my first flight on a chopper and I was fascinated by the view through the open hatch as we climbed into the sky.

LZ Carentan slipped away below us and I watched with a detached indifference as it grew smaller and finally disappeared. Carentan had been a village once, now abandoned it was our first combat staging area where all elements of the 11th Light Infantry Brigade gathered before spreading out all over Quang Ngai Province. Carentan was where war and death introduced themselves to us. I had just turned 23 and we had been in-country for two weeks with many more weeks ahead.

Rich Raitano at LZ Carentan (at right)

The convoy rolled into LZ Carentan in the mid-afternoon of December 20th, 1967, the day after we docked in Qui Nhon. Carentan was a sandy encampment, fidgety with the restless enthusiasm of thousands of soldiers settling into a warzone. Large numbers of local villagers under conical straw hats and wearing silk pajamas were everywhere. It was a queer sight, just as it was the day before in Qui Nhon, these people laboring within a military compound. There was much to learn.

Jim and I left our gear in our FLA (Front Line Ambulance) and headed for the aid station, which was nothing more than a big, army-green tent with most of our medical supplies stacked neatly to one side, waiting to be put in place. One by one the battalion medics arrived, and once we all were accounted for we discussed our next move.

It was decided that we should first erect the tent that would be our living quarters and let the organization of supplies wait until we were finished. Not having been tested by fire, we were having a good time laughing and joking while struggling with the construction of our new home. Our buoyant mood was more appropriate to a weekend camping trip than a combat encampment.

Deuce-and-a-halves filled with troops, and jeeps with officers, continued to roll in throughout the day sending billowing clouds of dust that covered our sweat-drenched bodies with a fine red powder. We were having one hell of a good time.

Once the tent was up and our cots were in place, we headed for the aid station and began the task of organizing our supplies and establishing an operational medical facility. We worked the rest of the evening and well into the night, and once everything was in place we retreated to our new home, talked for a while, and exhausted, drifted off to sleep.

The following two days, December 21st and 22nd, were spent filling sandbags and stacking them four feet high and two layers deep around the aid station and our quarters: blast walls to protect us from shrapnel and bullets. While we labored, Santa flew in on a Huey dressed in jungle fatigues, white beard and red cap, and handed candy-filled mesh Christmas stockings to each of us. It was surreal at best and left us all with thoughts of home and family.

Two medics had been picked to join one of the line companies on a local patrol early on the 22nd while the rest of us busied ourselves around the area and making rounds of the perimeter. All was relatively quiet those first days, except of course for the constant buzz of Hueys, the distant thunder of artillery, and muffled reports from a distant firefight. So far the war hadn't introduced itself. In the evening of December 22nd, sometime after dinner, a few of us wandered off to an isolated rise that put us slightly above our bivouac area and offered a clear view of the countryside.

It was easy to forget where we were. To our front, a large treeless hill rose in the near distance, and to the left, the rice paddies and open fields made a gentle incline towards a treeline, and beyond that, the mountains.

A joint appeared, was lit and passed around. A couple of Camel cigarettes were lit also and kept at the ready. We sat quietly, sucked in the harsh smoke and waited for the magical weed to entertain our brains.

A sudden muted burst to our left turned our heads in unison. Beyond the open fields, maybe three clicks away, a steady stream of tracers caught our eye. Two choppers were circling over a clearing and hurtling their hot death to the ground. Bright flashes of light followed seconds later by the booming report of explosive ordinance were turned into merriment by the cannabis frolicking in our heads. We were watching the war, in awe and completely indifferent to the mayhem taking place.

We heard someone approaching and quickly snuffed the weed and grabbed our Camels. PSGT Williams walked up, gazed back toward the clearing and turned again toward us. "You boys should get back to your units…" and with a knowing tone added…"Be careful." That was all he said, turned and left.

Later in that early star-filled morning of the 23rd, the beast came to pay us a visit. Charlie decided to test our mettle and hit the perimeter hard. The sudden and ferocious rattle of gunfire and ground-shaking explosions woke us abruptly from our sleep and thrust us into the reality of war. Someone, I think Bob, ran into the tent and called for medics. There were wounded on the perimeter and they needed FLAs…STAT!

I jumped up and grabbed my boots from under my cot, slipped them on and stuffed the laces inside. No time to lace and tie. The commotion in the dark tent sent us colliding into one another. I made it out and ran to my FLA, with Ralph right beside me headed for his FLA, and the two of us started our journey to the perimeter. The rest headed for the aid station.

Ralph and I made our way slowly to the perimeter where the fighting was in full fury, red night-driving lights softly illuminating the way. Stopped short of the wire by an anxious grunt, we grabbed our aid-bags and went the rest of the way on foot.

My heart was pounding hard in my chest and in my ears. Flares drifted crazily in the deep black sky, casting dizzying shadows on the ill-defined landscape beyond the wire. The crackling chatter of gunfire and violent roar of mortars and M-79 rounds grew louder as we made our way forward. Red and green tracers streaked back and forth from all directions like so many hurried fireflies. The tumbling buzz of hot, angry projectiles passed overhead and beside us. A sudden quick clank resounded behind us when a round hit an FLA.

Up to the wire and into the melee and confusion, we found our wounded. Ralph disappeared further down the perimeter and I picked up my patient. Another grunt assisted me getting him into the FLA, and once he was on board, I raced to the pad and waited for medevac.

He had gone out on a night training ambush led by Sgt. Maddox and they stumbled into a VC unit making its way toward our perimeter. A firefight erupted and Maddox went down. Godwin played dead as the VC moved over them and fired AK rounds into their prone bodies. Godwin was struck in the foot and continued to play dead while Charlie crawled over him.

Godwin's story was interrupted by the arrival of the Huey and I helped him onto the dust-off chopper and watched as it disappeared into the dark night. I made my way back to the perimeter and was told that all the casualties had been removed. The battle had subsided, but I was more than happy to head back to the aid station.

The assault had been a probe to test the unit's strength, and to identify weapon locations. It was an explosive event that had come and gone like a sudden summer thunderstorm. Perhaps the conflict we witnessed earlier had slowed this attack down.

I walked into the aid station, and in the dim light of lanterns, I saw several of our medics standing around a litter propped up on two sawhorses. A body lay on the litter. I was waved over and asked to join the group; our battalion doctor and company commander wanted us to see this dead man. His fatigue shirt had been opened exposing his chest and his pants had been removed. Edging closer, I saw that it was Maddox.

He had been shot several times and was covered in blood. One round left a gaping wound to his left cheek and tore away a piece of flesh, two rounds into his torso, and one into his thigh allowed the deep red of his blood to seep from his lifeless body. We were silent as we looked at this fallen man killed in combat. The realization of where we were had suddenly made its presence known to us.

Sgt Maddox had joined our brigade while we were still in Hawaii, three months before we shipped out. He had been in Viet Nam with the 1st Cav and was sent home on emergency leave. There had been a fire and two of his children had perished in the flames. His wife and one other child had survived. It is my understanding that he didn't have to ship out with us, but he insisted on returning to finish his tour.

And now he lay dead on a bloody litter, surrounded by army medics made to view his bullet-ridden body. Sgt Maddox was the battalion's first KIA, just four days after arriving in-country and one day after his twenty-fifth birthday.

It was unpleasant and unnerving to see this dead soldier. Our hearts still pounding and our senses yet raw, we stared at this man lying in a pool of his own blood. No amount of training prepared any of us for this moment. We stood there in stunned silence for what seemed like a very long time. This was not a movie or a field exercise, the man before us was dead and he was not coming back.

We were dismissed after half of us were picked to pull aid station duty while the rest of us went back to our tent. No one slept that night. A few days later five of us were chosen to relocate to LZ Sue.

LZ Sue (January 1968)

The chopper circled the saddle-shaped hill and made its gentle gliding approach. Several troops were standing near the pad as we touched down and began to offload. When we jumped from the bird, we came to understand that these troops were waiting to be ferried off the LZ; we were their replacements… FNGs. They looked tired, dirty; old for young men and each had a distant gaze that seemed to look through us. One grunt looked our way and uttered softly, but resolutely as he passed us, "Don't lose this fuckin' hill. A lot of good people died getting it."

Don't lose this fuckin' hill… a lot of good people died getting it.

That firm command has remained with me all these years. It was his severe demeanor and exhausted intensity that gave those words impact. Although not yet fully battle-tested, we had already experienced the grim results of war and understood his demand of us. There was no room for compromise. Men had been killed to claim this barren hill.

And so the baton was passed. But there was no dramatic orchestration to add melancholy emphasis to his words. No heroic dialogue. No proud and triumphant cheering. No polished military salute and snappy patriotic response. Just our bewildered stares and speechless thoughts greeted these weary veterans as they onloaded and floated away. Their presence was a profound warning. It was yet one more reminder that we were not out here to camp.

We were the next to last group to be dropped onto the LZ and Miller and I were the only medics on the hill. It was late in the day and the sun would be setting soon. We scrounged some C-rations and found a quiet spot near the perimeter.

We were high above a valley that swooped gently towards the deep purple mountains. A lazy river wound its way through trees, past the rice paddies and open fields. It was a beautiful sight in the fading daylight. Miller and I gathered up scrap wood pieces and built a small fire to warm our Cs. We were about five feet from the wire, talking low, enjoying the view, and eating our dinner.

Platoon Sgt Williams walked up to us with a casual "Howdy boys, how's it going?" We looked up at him, smiled; nodded and said things were fine. Nodding towards our little fire, he calmly said, "That's really not a good idea...", and looking past us and the wire he continued "...Charlie is out there."

Shit! What the hell were we thinking!? Once again we were lulled into the campout frame of mind, and once again PSGT Williams was our mentor. We quickly put the fire out and headed for the center of the hill where the safety of numbers seemed more acceptable and appropriate, and far enough from the truth of the wire.

The sun had set and it was nearly dark. We chose to crawl under the communications trailer for the night, perceiving it to be a safe place. In the waning light, our duffle bags passing as pillows and our M-16s by our side, we struggled with the Viet Nam reality. It was early January, 1968. *Welcome to Viet Nam, boys.*

TET

TET Nguyen Dan is the celebration of the Vietnamese New Year and is considered to be an important holiday in Viet Nam. It is a celebration of Spring and the beginning of a new year. It is a time for family reunions, and exchanging gifts. A combination of Thanksgiving, Christmas, New Year's, and everyone's birthday rolled into one event; even the ancestors are welcomed into the homes to participate in the festivities.

Having had a cease-fire on Christmas Day we expected no less for TET. The night of January 31st, 1968 proved otherwise. Some time in the middle of the night we were awakened by the explosive concussion of incoming mortar rounds. Grabbing our M-16s and flak jackets—and throwing our helmets on—we quickly vacated our bunkers and made for the aid station.

It was pitch black and the way was briefly lit by the lightning flashes of each round as it pummeled our base. *Crrumpph. Crrumpph-crrumph...*each thundering report throwing debris and shrapnel in every direction. Hearts pounding, and fear stuck in our throats, we raced into the aid station. Three of us were sent to the artillery position. An incoming round had landed near the ammo dump and ignited a case of charges; wounding three and severely burning another.

We grabbed a litter and quickly made our way to the Arty position and the wounded. We met them at the helipad coming up to our position. Setting the badly injured man on the litter, we made our way back to the aid station; mortar rounds still falling.

Once in the aid station we saw the extent of the burned man's injuries. His clothes were charred and smoking and the skin on his face, hands and arms hung from him, his wounds raw and glistening. He was in a high state of anxiety and going into shock. We set his litter on a sawhorse and our doctor began to attend to him. He repeatedly asked if he was going to be OK and although we really didn't know, we assured him that he was just fine.

While the doctor treated him, we treated his buddies and left to make the rounds of the LZ. The barrage had stopped but we could still see distant flashes all around us as the attack was still under way; one huge flash lit up the sky when the fuel dump in Chu Lai was hit.

Although no longer under attack, we remained on high alert all through the night. Fortunately no one had been killed, and only a handful had been wounded that night. We received the news several days later that our burn patient had died at the American Military hospital in Japan.

The North Vietnamese Army and Vietcong had launched coordinated attacks at nearly every military installation and LZ in South having violated the pledge to observe a truce, they had managed to catch both South Vietnamese and American forces off guard.

The TET Offensive was totally unexpected. While it may have been a "tactical failure" in that there had been no major defeat of American or ARVN (South Vietnamese) forces, the swift and co-coordinated attack was a "strategic success." It very well may have been the event that caused support for the war in the United States to begin its slide downward and led to the torturously slow American withdrawal from Vietnam.

We estimated that somewhere between twenty and twenty-five rounds fell on us that night, many falling short of the perimeter. It was a hell of a night all across Viet Nam.

13 Poetry

Preston Hood

At The Wall

I've seen it before, etched in the faces of men who have gone to war: through Gods they speak, whirlwinds of bloodlust & grief. And I recall while dying—an eagle gliding upside down into the horizon, the sun gold & dusking—the late afternoon of a long autumn in the mountains—the burnt leaves blowing.

Slowly I begin to let go of daily & nightly sorrow, of loss—then midstep—I'm huddled in dense fog near a pond, strange person to myself. In death throes, I see the front door... swinging, filling space with light, spinning. The planet I live on drops like a tossed coin in a fountain. *Where am I? Am I really here? Do I exist?*

I tackle the smaller idea first. The larger one hits me with its darkness, a conception the impression I'm hurting of, axes out my soul; I fear the silence of footsteps sneaking up. Sorrow's shadow buried along with bulldozed feelings. Death is a shotgun fired through the heart: Loss corners you after the killing, a rat, eating.

What I know is that sometimes the surf breaks into shredded moonlight ribbon. Above me the inky clouds hold sky's weight. The open seas are an amber haze one morning become a straight line to indifference. I want you to know that I am sixty-four & recently started living.

Marc Levy

Dead Letter Day

He sent the letter to the guy's wife
The same day,
Leaving out the following:
"About two in the morning the automatic went off
And nobody moved, we just waited for the morning
Light and the order to recon.
There were two of them. One was dead.
The other hung on all night,
Waiting to blow away some round-eyes
Before he bought it too.
He shot the second man, missing the point.
The point opened up and somebody threw a frag
And it was all over. Except that your husband
Took a bullet through his helmet that tore a
Gash in his head, and going down shot the man
In front of him. The blood was deep, dark red;
He was lying flat on his back, in shock;
His eyes were wide-open and lifeless,
As if he could see everything.
They say he lived a few days in the rear,
Even got up and spoke. Then died.
Head wounds are like that."
She wrote back. First thanking him and the platoon
For writing her, then going on for pages asking
About his last moments. You could tell she was crying;
And he cried too, and did not reply to the desperate
Letter, and has desperately not replied ever since.

---

automatic: an American booby trap
round-eye(s): Americans
point: the first man in a patrol

Alan Farrell

On Catching Sight of an M-188 Tracked Recovery Vehicle Recovering an M-188 Tracked Recovery Vehicle

My colonel and I amble across the dustdry Haute Région compound
One step left and one step uncovered militarycourtesy
I'm slinging his piece and mine both muzzledown
Barbedwiretangles
Cokecanlidspangles
Plaintive windjangles
   in this warm Highland air

At the entrance to camp sloughing skin like a viper
Sandbag wall sinks under the weight of its futility
The Old Man pauses to have a word with the *bru* gateguard
Tooserious little sage
Fatigues bleached beige
Skin taut without age
   in this warm Highland air

Comes now rumbling up *QL Fourteen* a spectral juggernaut
An chaste coupling of monsters unclean joining of corpulent casting
An M-188 Tracked Recovery Vehicle
     r
        e
           c
              o
                  v
                     e
                        r
                           s
        another M-188 Tracked Recovery Vehicle
Remorseless loop of churning treads
Roaddustwhisker threads
Clay highway now shreds
   in this warm Highland air

The Old Man and I stare blankly first at the lumbering apparitions
Then he at me and I at him in a moment of common recovery
A dark epiphany deep and resonant and ineffable and horrid
A glimpse of Fate
Of Irony at any rate
From the 'yard camp gate
   In this warm Highland air

Some noface echelon sent those galumphing oxen diesel of the unblinking Asian sun
The first to haul out a wounded track some mudsucked ACAV
The second to retrieve the first when he, too, couldn't wouldn't didn't
And so on ad infinitum
Too many to cite 'em
Item after inventoriedsurveyedstackedstockedstuckendless item
   in this warm Highland air

The team to recover the man and the squad to recover them and now
The platoon to recover the squad and a company to recover them and then
A batallion them a Division them and another 250,000 sonsabitches to recover us sonsabitches
A mortal refrain
No use to complain
Maybe it'll rain
   in this warm Highland air.

Tom Skiens

Rally Round the Flag, Boys

In a dream
On a day
We walk together
This way
Absolute perfection
A light
A walk, a smile
Harmonious precision
In tune, on time
A fear
A dread to come
A tear
First to drop the bomb

I have this strange feeling
On the Persian Gulf thing
My emotions on edge
Long tight-rope, narrow string

It's like standing in a black cloud
A dark and hollow place
I focus on tomorrow's events
I wonder of the human race

We balance on the brink of war
It seems just a matter of time
The solider again as cannon fodder
I have visions of dead and dying

I'm filled with the pain of knowing
Of having been through it all before
While I deal with a post-war trauma
A new war knocks on the door

Oh rally round the flag boys
We're on a presidential high
Either love it now or leave it
Don't question right just die

Oh rally round the flag boys
Send your neighbor's son to war
Talk loud with threats to kick some ass
Let's see some blood and gore

Oh rally round the flag boys
Send your best friend's wife to fight
Call up the Reserves and National Guard
The President says he is right

Oh rally round the flag boys
Hold old glory way up high
Watch it flutter in the breeze
As coffins pass slowly by

Oh rally round the flag boys
Call up the Viet Nam Vets
This time we'll win the war so fast
We'll kill with no regrets

Oh rally round the flag boys
The peace-freaks damned to hell
Mark your targets, squeeze and breathe
Please salivate at the sound of the bell

Oh rally round the flag boys
Fight till the fighting's done
Then reject the ones who risk their life
Take away their knives and guns

Oh rally round the flag boys
Deny the horror and the pain
The nightmare's watching your friends die
Again and again and again

Oh rally round the flag boys
Huddle close and hear me say
Fight this war to end all wars
Except the ones that haunt your days

Dayl Wise

Ode to the P-38

No, not the P-38 Lightning aircraft,
nor German semi-automatic pistol.
You're a field ration can opener,
Officially:
Opener "*comma*",
Can "*comma*",
Hand "*comma*",
Folding "*comma*",
Type I.

You're were small and light to carry,
Hinged, nickel-plated, hardened steel,
cheap, petite, 1-1/2 inches long.

You adorned my dog tag chain,
like a ring, my steady.
Around the block a few times,
WWII, Korea. With me... Vietnam.

Environmentally friendly,
light weight,
you're human-powered,
no batteries for you.

Opened C-rations, bottles,
stripped wire, cleaned boots,
fingernails, a great marking tool.
Once scaled a fish. Do you remember?

We parted that fall night, 24th Evac Hospital,
my last vision of you, around my neck.
Resting on my dog tags,
never saw you again.

I think of you often my love,
but we both knew it was temporary.
Heard about your retirement,

with the adoption of MREs.

Thank you for everything,
for penetrating all those C-rats.
Never been able to bring myself
to buy an electric can opener.

March 3, 2008

MREs: Meals Ready-to-Eat, individual field ration in lightweight packaging.
C-rats: Nickname for C-rations containing a canned entrée, three cans containing cheese, crackers, candy, a dessert and cigarettes.

Dayl Wise

Ode to boots

You covered my feet,
you weathered over time,
a badge of field experience.
No spitshine tip to look into,
no reflection of that lost child.
Your laces always tight,
A mother's knot.

How far did we travel
before they cut you off?
Others came home,
not you, discarded
like a pair of unwanted slippers
piled in a bloody heap
of clothing and bone.

April 1, 2008

Marc Levy

14   **Torque in Angkor Wat**

I am fortunate. I have no problems with highly charged emotional states. No past events which I cannot discuss. I am lucky. I do not struggle with feelings of loss, feelings of guilt, anger, flashbacks, nightmares. I sleep well. I do not toss or kick or leg cramp or leap at ghosts. I am fortunate. I have not one splinter of conflict within me.

There are two of us in the great tan field of withered grass. It is the heat and drought that have done it. Everywhere the sun disk kills with its merciless light. Only the surrounding jungle, which lords over buried ruins, the leafy sheltering jungle which may harbor unsavory men, only the effervescent green canopy provides shade, here at Preah Khan.

I am wearing faded blue-jeans, a white T-shirt and hiking boots. I am thin. It is easy to lose weight back packing and I have lost 30 pounds in four months. At 46, I am lithe and muscular. My thick hair is jet black. I'm told I look young for my age. I'm told there are no lines on my face because I do not smile. Often I say to myself "What do they know?" and I say it without malice.

In Cambodia marijuana is sold in open-air markets at five dollars per kilo. It is not uncommon to see young tourists huff on long, thick joints. I do not smoke or drink or take drugs, but Jack does.

Jack is an engine of madness. He envies me. Jack wanted war and did not go and knows I did and pretends he doesn't care. In this way we continue the game, the one in our sweaty heads, the other, the Frisbee, which arcs like a rocket between us.

Jack is built like an iron bull. His broad shoulders frame a massive chest with twin pectoral shields; he is narrow-waisted; his abdomen is a ladder of muscle. His arms and legs are taut and firm. A square jaw juts a manly cleft chin. Beneath the pummeling sun his steely eyes glow in their sockets. He is fast, agile, cat-like.

Jack has smoked and drank and worked his body for ten years and today the red dragon tattoo which spans his proud chest breathes salty fire in the hot, sweet air.

We are standing fifty meters apart. When Jack wings the Frisbee it cuts a well-placed bullet path into my waiting hands. My hands which are bleeding and blistered.

"Nice throw," I say.

Jack is astonished when I pivot and catch the energetic disk behind my back. He cannot believe it. I am ten years his senior. But I have killed, saved and lost men. I have the papers and medals to prove it.

Poor Jack. Poor well-built, swagger-walk, shaven-head, glow-eyed, stoned-cold Jack cannot believe my prowess.

"You're damn good," he says. "You're really damn good."

When I toss the dancing circle so well, so finely placed he need not move, not budge, not shift one inch to catch it, he is doubly astonished.

"Christ," he says.

Here is how we met:

The speedboat from Phnom Penh to Angkor Wat cost twenty-one dollars and took five hours. Inside, the long sleek craft is crowded with double rows of tourists. Many are drunk. They laugh, sing, and frolic. Others are sleeping, lulled by the constant roar of the boat's turbo engines. I am kept awake by loudspeakers hooked to the walls which blare American rock music throughout the stuffy cabin. After an hour the noise makes me crazy. I walk up a narrow stairway and sit in one of two canvas chairs near the stern. The boat scuds forward on the Tunnele Sap River; its pitch-dark water sprays my body and pelts my face. It feels good to be alive.

Soon another passenger, Jack, joins me. Bare-chested, he is wearing military rip-stop cargo pants. His blond hair is cut short and white-walled. As he walks the boat's roof he instinctively sways with the watery rhythm. By the way he steps, by the way he seats himself, drops his lean body into the sun-bleached chair, he exudes confidence. He exudes manliness. I do not ask about the furious dragon with its rolling eyes and scaly skin and whip like tail. After a time we speak.

"Yes, yes. I look too young but I was there and war is a terrible thing. It plays tricks on your mind," I say. "It changes you. But now we're in Cambodia and it's 1995." When I become emotional Jack looks away. Then I regain my poise and he tells me his story.

Jack enlisted in 1976 after one year of college. Infantry. Jump school. Special Forces. "Why?" I ask. Jack says his brother lost both legs in Viet Nam. "Both legs," he repeats. Jack wanted revenge, but the Army said no. After a time he re-trained as a cook, and never left Fort-Carson.

For three years Jack griddles stuffed omelets, molds pastries, fancy breads, extracts the blood from immense raw steaks. For three long years he is undone by the clatter of cups, the clink of dishes, by white linen draped over smooth wood tables. Off-duty he immerses himself in karate. He learns to kill with one punch and during this time seeks conflict in dark GI bars and bright public places. He is arrested many times. He has never lost a fight. When it is time to go he is honorably discharged with all rank and benefits despite his poor conduct. But Jack has obtained no medals, no battle scars, only minor bar room bruises. When I explain his good fortune Jack pretends to listen as the sea-wind buffets our faces and cools our bodies.

As he tells me his story the hours pass and the boat slows to enter a small narrow channel. Thin, tense Cambodian sailors man American gunboats armed with heavy machine guns which are cocked and ready. The thin men come close then step aboard to inspect passenger documents.

"Pass-port. Pass-port," they say, stressing the syllables.

The Cambodians are wearing French camouflage uniforms and Chinese steel helmets. They carry AKs and M-16s and smooth American grenades. Frags, we called them. Some passengers take pictures but the sailors shoo them away, as if they are scolding children. Then the sailors are gone. When our boat pulls to shore we are met by a legion of nervous soldiers who form a phalanx through which we pass.

It begins raining a cold, piercing rain which turns the dark earth to chill muddy soup. The passengers, mostly young foreign backpackers freighted with too much clothing and gear slip and slide and look for shelter. Soon they panic. Only Jack and I remain calm. We make a gallant path through the fumbling amateurs. For some reason the frightened youth and well-armed men make way. We step with authority, we step forward as if we know this ground.

The driver of the idling truck is a middle-aged man, his caramel face pitted by a hundred stories that would take a lifetime to tell. He wears simple, common clothes; he wears a red-and-white checkered Cambodian scarf around his neck. When he speaks I watch the rise and fall of his jugular vein, which is thick with blood.

"Me take you to finest guest house," he says through a bridge of rotted teeth.

At first I never killed anyone. The machine gunners and riflemen did that. I carried morphine and bandages to ease their pain. The first dead American I saw was black. Then I helped in the killing. And the killing helped me.

It is cold and damp inside the rusting American military truck. Jack nods his approval. I lower my chin. There is war in my mouth and it tastes like bullets. I am silent. Then we are off. In the blinding downpour rain pelts the windshield in thunderous beats which makes sight impossible. I expect the last-minute swerve, the grind of gears, the screech of brakes, the slow-motion fragmenting glass as our bodies pass through it. But the driver grips the wheel with one hand and repeatedly ducks his head out the side window, squinting and shaking and steering all at once. Soon he is thoroughly wet. Water drips round the sacred curve of his large Cambodian ears. It drips down the well-worn path made by his venerable cheek bones and triangular jaw. It drips into the red-white checkered scarf softly knotted around his throat. Water gathers and drifts down his lean torso, down his meager Asian hairless legs, down his delicate bare feet, until finally it pools itself onto the rotted steel floor and sinks to the flooded road beneath us.

In our wild dash through the broad and narrow streets of Siem Reap, as we glide and splash through submerged roads that crest like rivers, the pulsate drip, drip, drip of solitary water beads makes me calm.

"Here is guest house," says our driver, pointing toward a rain-swept path.

We pay with wet money and rush outside. By the time we enter the clean, dry, well-lit room our clothes are drenched. Jack removes his shirt, seats himself at a wide yellow sofa, and busies himself in the crimp and curl of joints. I remain standing and silent and he thinks I'm strange. I say I'm cold and tired. I say perhaps tomorrow we'll visit Angkor Wat. Jack says "Sure" and I say goodnight. An ageless friendly woman emerges from a glass bead door. She parts it with her hands locked in prayer.

"Here key," she says, accepting money.

In my large room with its square thick bed and vault of mosquito netting I take pills and lie down and do not recall my dreams. Before sleep I tell myself I am good, I am calm, I am strong.

This is how it works: they walk into us, we walk into them, we walk into each other. Oh, there is magic in these moments. Magic in the mannered step of patrol, ambush, jungle, monsoon. Magic in the machine gun's vile abracadabra. Magic in the illusory arc of seamless tracers. Wizardry in the rampaging men who run, crouch, advance, explode. Oh, there is infinite wit and timely jest in the ten thousand ways men hunt and kill. Survival. That is the sacred trick of war. That is the heart of it. The obscene and secret center.

In the morning Jack and I flag down a weather-beaten motorcycle. It is a strange sight: two large men gathered around one thin man whose fragile machine we must commandeer to visit eternal Angkor Wat. In the banter of bargain the gaunt Cambodian stands his ground and we call his bluff by leaving.

"OK. OK," he shouts. "Five dollah for both. Five dollah."

A small fortune in a country where once a life could be lost for the crime of wearing glasses.

We straddle the slim seat and, bunched up, hold tight to flimsy belts.

"You ready? You ready?"

"Yes," we shout in unison.

The driver races down long empty boulevards flanked by massive leafy trees which make the morning air bright and cool. Only the sputtering engine breaks the invisible silence. Ghosts are nearby, I know it, I can feel them.

When we reach the great sprawling temple we are dumbstruck. The long pale building snakes across the horizon like a sideways totem spirit caught in the dream-world between rest and waking. The strange organic stone palace beckons us forward. For three long hours we inhabit the intricate site. Stepping like deer over the white stone floors, we honor the warrior carvings. The driver grows impatient.

"All right," we say, and ride to a temple where the jungle has not been slashed and burned and cleared away.

"This Ta'Prom," says our driver. As we dismount he wipes sweat from his brow and beneath his breath utters the strange words "Khmer Rouge."

Jack tells him to wait by the side of the road and we begin walking forward. I look about. Where have I seen these great twisty vines, sky-poking trees, dirt trails studded by jagged rocks cocooned in pillows of emerald moss? Where did I first hear the animate sounds of green triple-canopy traced with decay and life? I want to run, I want to hide, I want to plummet childlike into this vast room of living dreams.

But the sweltering heat makes us lazy. We drink rivers of bottled water and take refuge in lichen-covered stone temples where all colors are sublime. I sit and talk with a small boy selling souvenirs. Jack takes photographs, then hunkers down and smokes a paper stick while seated bunched up like a gargoyle.

Idiot, I want to say. We are guests to a lost age in sacred rooms which know the luminous voice of prayer and song. We are guests under low roofs locked in the vise of towering trees and serpentine vines. We are surrounded by stone and light and triple-layered jungle which knows no law but its own. Idiot, I want to say. Can you not feel each living moment tick past? Can you not know what it's like to live here? What it means to rush forward to the screaming men? Idiot, I want to say, can't you taste and smell the humans veiled in billowing cordite? Can't you see the frozen man who cannot move? In war the living become like statues lifted by helicopters, or left to decay. Silly, wasted idiot. Do you not know what it's like to wake from a monstrous dream still swallowed in sprawling nightmare?

See how the impartial sun fills me with fear. See how the percussive white hammer spits metal through skin. See how I freeze decades after the event.

Dear stoned wasted one: In war all suffer their fates. I am fortunate: The dead do not speak when I talk back. Or judge my sins. Look at you smoking your tight-rolled reveries. What do you know?

It is our third day at Angkor Wat. Jack knows I will meet him later. I have risen early, hoisted my pack and sped to a deserted point behind Ta'Prom. In the lustrous emerald shelter I unfold the once-green nylon hammock still stained by red dirt. Automatically, my eyes measure the distance for its still strong rope. Automatically, my fingers loop square knots to the center of trees; my hands adjust the hammock to hang just above the ground, the better to roll out in case of attack. But there are only flies and leeches and the jungle's slow organic crawl. I smear insect repellent on my hands, on my arms, and face. I straddle the embracing nylon sheet, then sit, then lie straight back. I am running; I am hiding; I am plunging full-force into the dream. The book I have brought falls from my hand.

At dusk, after we form a perimeter with trip-flares, dig foxholes, plant mines; after we have eaten, after we have checked our weapons, drawn matchsticks for guard, I lay in a small area cleared with a knife borrowed from a friend who will die in two weeks. In the middle of night a new man nearly steps on my face. "You're guard," he says, setting the bulky radio down before disappearing into the inky black.

I crawl to the foxhole. Its warm wet walls are studded with quick-cut roots which bleed clear sap. An hour goes by. A voice whispers over the radio, "If your sitreps are negative break squelch twice." But my situation report is not negative. Twenty, thirty meters ahead I hear the soft graze of cloth on twigs. I hear the tell-tale rise and push of rubber sandaled feet on the green-matted jungle floor. Huddled down, I squeeze the detonator and the mine explodes. A great white flash and metallic bang fill the air. For a moment they are visible. Then there is running and small-arms fire and someone explodes a second mine. Boom! Now they are screaming. The machine gunners seek out survivors. In the morning we find blood trails and human meat. Save for one they have dragged away their dead. The frail human sculpture trapped in rags is riddled with bullets. The pith helmet beside her is torn to shreds. Her weapon is mangled and useless. It is she who wept and groaned all night; it is she whose pleading voice haunts us as we scavenge her pockets.

When I wake the sun is directly overhead. It is time to move out. Time to march to the field. I untie knots, coil the rope, spread the hammock flat on the ground, fold it lengthwise in half and roll it up, hoist my pack, and begin walking. It is a good twenty-minute hike on a well-used trail. The last three words have special meaning. I scan for footprints, heel marks dragged backwards. Automatically I bob and sway and keep to the side; I am searching for men who lie in wait. But there is nothing. Only the tranquil path and flitting birds and unforbidding jungle. The mimic of memory. That is what most annoys me, what Jack cannot comprehend: When I see or smell or feel things that are not there. For every step of the next mile I tell myself I am strong, I am calm, I am good.

"Christ," says Jack.

We continue playing. He whips the flying ring across the flat, dead field. I catch it left-handed, or between my legs, or with eyes closed, whatever it takes to heighten the risk. The day burns bright with heat and I want to be 10,000 times more powerful than Jack, who grins at each weapon-like exchange. He presses a joint to his lips between turns. The plastic wheel sings like a bullet between us.

Suddenly behind Jack, nine young Cambodian troops emerge from the treeline. Their uniforms are ripped and filthy; their silent sandals are made from tires banded by strips of inner-tube; tight-knotted red bandanas encircle their bushy heads. They wield a motley patchwork of AK-47s, shoulder-fired RPGs, a weary American machine gun. Yes. They have been hunting Khmer Rouge. Beads of sweat roll down their gaunt faces which they mop with the backs of their filthy hands. I watch as their black almond eyes track the dancing disk sweeping over the dry tan field. Their expression is unreadable.

Seeing a curious look on my face, Jack turns around. After a moment he slings the Frisbee to an older man who appears in charge. The man fumbles the catch and annoyed throws it back. It is a weak throw and he is clearly troubled. Jack laughs, then trots up to another soldier, man or woman it is hard to say, and offers the joint. The Cambodians uneasily share it, and Jack cannot control his laughter. He is slapping his sides. He is bent over double. In six puffs the paper wand evaporates but the Cambodians raise their weapons and point them at Jack. He finds this hilarious and laughs even louder.

Walking forward I stare straight into the Cambodians' blood raging eyes. Howling with laughter, Jack picks up the Frisbee and tosses it to me. But I don't want to see it. Where are the foxholes? Where are the Claymore mines? Where are the weapons and knives and radio? The war is everywhere and Jack is blind to it.

He continues to laugh. He thinks the forced grin on my face is reciprocal laughter. He thinks I have come to pick up the plastic wheel that has fallen at my trekking-boot feet. He thinks I walk toward him and the seething group to bow to the triumph of the joke in a halo of sweat. But when I reach Jack I throw the hardest punch of my life and he drops like a burlap bag filled with red dirt and does not move. Straightening up, I lock eyes with each Cambodian. The commander nods. The others lower their weapons. Then like mist they dissolve into the jungle.

I spoke to Jack as he lay there jaggedly jawed, the dead grass beneath him stippled red. Strange words flew from my mouth. I spoke non-stop and the words sounded fierce in a language I don't remember.

On the boat back to Phnom Penh I recalled the startled look in Jack's eyes. What had he seen and what did he know? Over the time it took to re-cross the Tunnele Sap River, I realized it didn't matter.

I continued traveling. Some days were good, some were bad. But I swear that I never, not once in all the hectic times that followed, whatever the country wherever I laid my head, did I ever look back. Like a river I am always moving forward.

Sitrep: (Situation Report) a regular communications check between units in the field and the rear

Pieter van Aggelen

15   A South African in Viet Nam

The following transcript is from Robert Moore's radio show which aired in March 1990. His guest is Pieter van Aggelen, a South African national who fought for the US in Viet Nam.

Robert Moore (RM): We are going to be talking about the experience of a fellow who went to Viet Nam and came back with a problem. That problem which is commonly known as PTSD—Post Traumatic Stress Disorder. I had an opportunity to hear you tell your story in San Francisco at a TIR-related conference and I would like to have you have the opportunity to share your experience with my audience

Pieter van Aggelen (PvA): I'm going to start in a chronological fashion as to who I am, so you can get a bit of an understanding about me. I was born in the republic of South Africa and my father was in the banking business and moved between various countries a lot. At the age of thirteen, I moved to Europe and spent eighteen months on vacation so to speak, then moved to New York City in 1964. I was not told that we were leaving our home, which was Johannesburg. I heard it on board the Queen Mary as we passed the Statue of Liberty. My father walked up and said "Oh by the way, you know we're never going home." That did not sit well with me and I was rather angry with not being told. Our relationship went downhill from there.

Here I was on holiday, I had not gone to school for eighteen months and I was not looking forward to learning American history. I was a teenager then, around fourteen and half years old. I straight into the American school system. It was kind of a difficult time for me, because I had not really been exposed to racism nor was I a racist. In school people were reading Paton's *Cry the Beloved Country* and *Black Like Me* and everybody would always turn to Pieter and say "What do you think of that?" I found that a little difficult, but I managed to get over that.

By the time I turned age seventeen, I was quite unhappy. One of the things I thought of doing was running away from home. I spoke to a neighbor, who was a clergyman, and he suggested maybe it would be a good idea to join the service as I was rather young. Even though I was still not an American citizen, I could still fight for the US.

I went to a delicatessen right after I spoke to the minister and met a gentleman named Staff Sgt Billy Jay Tiller who was the Marine Corps recruiter and decked-out in his dress blues. The minister advised me to wait until I was eighteen and had graduated high school and then join the military. But, this man told me I could join at seventeen.

Within days, I had talked to my parents. My mother was willing, but my father was not. He had been a Japanese POW for four years and he didn't think he wanted me to do that. He wanted me to become a banker. It was worked out and the papers were signed. Within a month after turning seventeen, I was in Parris Island, South Carolina. It was April 1966, just before the war was really starting to heat up and I was aware of that. My mother had told me that anyone who missed a war missed one of the most important things in life—because I could learn a lot from that.

Although I would eventually serve the standard Marine tour of thirteen months in-country, I did not head out there directly from Parris Island. Instead, I was sent to Washington, DC as an honor guard and given special security clearance and so I thought that I was somehow chosen as special. But the fact was, as I found out many years later, that I was only seventeen and they couldn't ship me directly to Viet Nam with the rest of the people. A new law had been passed recently that they could no longer send seventeen year-olds. [Ed. Note: the average age of soldiers in Viet Nam was nineteen.]

So I did my stint in Washington and as soon as I turned eighteen, and along with almost my entire guard detachment of 31 people, got a 30-day leave before being shipped off to Viet Nam. First, however, we went to California for some hot-weather training and then we were flown to Da Nang via Anchorage and Okinawa. Our group was immediately broken up within a few hours of landing at Da Nang airport. A few of us from our guard detachment were sent to 3rd Battalion, 7th Marines. A truck picked us up and we were issued M-16 rifles, but no magazines or bullets.

We had to go out to our unit, which was about seventeen miles as the crow flies. But it turned out to be a twisty 30 mile trip with a 50-caliber machine gun mounted on top of the truck just blasting away at every bush as we went, to avoid ambushes. We drove 60 miles per hour because if there was a road mine, this would save the driver in the event of an explosion (those of us riding in the truckbed would not be saved). It was a very unsettling experience.

From there we went to Lima Company and I was given a bandolier of magazines, which I had to load myself. Then they took four of us out in a small armored personnel carrier to try out our new M-16s. We fired two or three magazines into a bush and were considered ready, even though we had not been properly trained.

I was then walked to a bridge where there were about eight fellows sitting in bunkers on either side. This was to be my squad and there I was. It was very strange because nobody spoke to me when I arrived, they just looked at my suspiciously. When it got dark that evening, one of the fellas passed me what looked like a thin home-rolled cigarette. And then I smiled and said "Oh, I've got Winstons from the US". They all looked at me like "What are you crazy? This is a joint." At that point they got this look, like: where did this kid come from?

I was extremely afraid after a little while when they asked me about my previous duty station, which was Washington, DC. Was I possibly from Official Naval Investigations? One fellow told me to, "Smoke it or you might not make it." So I took a few hits on the joint. Everybody calmed down being reassured that I was not ONI.

The implication was that something bad would happen to me. The way these people were looking at me, I felt like my life was in danger. If they didn't trust you, you were gone, which I found out later. In any case, that night I took a few hits on a joint and it was one of the most abhorrent things I had done in my life up to that point. But I soon learned to get over that.

I did not become a regular user, but I did smoke on occasion as an escape. Once I understood why people smoked, I basically made it my business not to mind anybody else's business. It was a very dangerous thing to do that.

I had now been assigned to a squad. On the next day, I went on my first patrol. Our squads were usually six or seven people. We would go out and you have basically a point man, a corporal in charge of the platoon (I was a Private First Class at that point), and somebody with an M-79 grenade launcher, and a couple of other riflemen. You would go and walk around in what was called our Tactical Area of Responsibility (TAOR). We would be given orders each day to go to different areas. We would go out for a morning patrol, do an afternoon patrol, and then take out a night-ambush. After I had been in that situation for about two days, I realized that the people who had been doing point man walking up front were not paying attention like I would have with my experience as a kid with hunting and tracking in the jungles of South Africa. I volunteered to take over that position and did so for nine months.

There is always the question as to whether the point man, as the guy up front, is at the greatest risk. Some guys feel that way, I don't. The one thing that the point is able to do is that he can go to a specific area the way that *he wants to go*. Especially at night, because nobody is going to be shouting "Hey Pieter, go to the left" or what to do or how to get there because your legs are going to get blown off if you step on a mine. That was something that was left to the point man. You basically could go whichever way you wanted to. I would not walk into an ambush, I was known as lucky on that. I walked point and most people abhorred doing that, but I preferred that to having anybody walk me into anything. Another thing, the point man usually would go through before the ambush was sprung. There also, I figured I had an edge on.

RM: I see, so the tactic was to let the column pass and nail it from behind?

PvA: Or nail it from the side. I usually used to stay well out ahead, 50 or 100 yards if possible. That gave me an opportunity to at least get down behind cover when the ambush was sprung, because I'm not the one with the M-79 grenade launcher or the backpack-sized radio. Those guys were a lot more bunched up than I was out in front.

RM: So they were less interested in the point than the rest of the column?

PvA: Definitely, that's something that I figured out very quickly. Then we would have operations which were large units where we would get three or four companies of Marines (500 or more men in the field). We would be picked up by helicopter with 30 to 60 minutes' notice and be taken over to an area where reconnaissance reported large North Vietnamese base camps. We would sweep the areas to try and find them. It was usually done with an anvil procedure where one company would be put forward as bait.

On these major operations, one thing which became clear very quickly was that nobody really seemed to know what they were doing, what the mission was, or where they were at any particular point in time. I had a good friend—which was a rarity—a lieutenant who contacted me on his arrival because he had heard I was an outstanding point, to show him the area. On operation, I would get to hear quite a bit of what was going on because I would walk point for my platoon sometimes or in fact most of the time. One thing which was clear: when we called artillery (which was not very often), we did not know where we were. That was true of everyone, regardless of the level.

We had maps but nobody quite knew most of the time or even half the time exactly where we were on the map because the maps were not as good as we would like them to be. One hill, looking at it, looked very much like another hill and there were no signs on anything.

RM: From this and your prior presentation in San Francisco, I take it there was a high degree of disorganization.

PvA: It not only appeared that way, it was that way. The idea of when we were looking for the enemy and there would be four or five square miles of open rice paddies, that they would put 200 men on line and walk across that to sweep them. What we knew was that there would be snipers a few miles away on hills with long range rifles. They were going to wait for us to get in the middle and then they would shoot a few people. We would get the command to "charge" where we thought the gunfire came from, of course not knowing. We would just go running off to secure the area, call in the medevac, and then the sniper would open up again on the medevac.

You would get into these nasty tangled affairs on a daily basis where nothing seemed to get accomplished. People's frustration and anger just built daily, because we never got contact with enemy. They would always slip away, we would come across trenches and fortifications with their home-rolled cigarettes still burning. They were always gone, but we would always run into snipers and booby-traps. It just really seemed like nothing was getting done.

RM: Is this typical of the conduct of war historically or is there something new or different here from Korea or WWII?

PvA: Well, I think that one of the major problems was that it was based on a lot of lies. For instance on body-counts, when some of our people got shot, our lieutenant would walk around and say "Well, how many did you get today?" You would say "I only got three" and someone else said "I only got four" and he would make up the list. When in actual fact, none of us had shot anybody in the way of an enemy. Then he would call that into the captain. Then the captain would hear from another company who had more casualties. He would then call that into the colonel and those figures would go to Marble Mountain in Da Nang and be compiled. By the time we got through with the war, we had killed the entire population of North and South Viet Nam several times over.

Basically, I think what the people in the rear were sitting quietly listening to wasn't true. A lot of the intelligence that we had was subverted. As happened on Operation Foster [March 1967], a laundrywoman who would wash my clothes in the river inadvertently tipped me off that the intelligence had been broken. Before this incident, I been taught by someone not to pay my entire laundry bill at once, that you should always leave five dollars on the tab. This woman came up to me one day and demanded "You pay money now, you going to go on buck-buck VC on Thursday". This was Monday.

RM: What did that mean?

PvA: She wanted to be paid before Thursday, therefore she had the schedule for Operation Foster. I went to Mac, my lieutenant, and he said "No, I've heard nothing." He went and checked and also heard nothing. On Thursday, we got the call, "Saddle up, you're going on operation." Those things are commonplace from what I've heard from other veterans who spoke some Vietnamese and got along a bit. It seems that it was run very poorly. When we got to these areas, they certainly through some means had advance notice that we were coming.

RM: I can appreciate the confusion you are describing. Considering that you developed PTSD later, the impression that I get is that you were doing pretty well at staying out of trouble to a considerable extent.

PvA: I did stay out of trouble, except when I would get angry. That I would keep under cuffs for most of the time. About operations, what really set me off was when we heard a radio call from a little plane called a Bird Dog (Cessna O-1) that the pilot had seen at least 500 of the enemy out in the open. We were all cheering.

I had an argument with a Staff Sergeant about how many people should go out and set up down by a lake. I had a premonition and sure enough about three or four minutes later the jets arrived. We saw the F-111s coming in, these little black dots at first, there were three of them.

They made their circle as I was standing and talking to lieutenant McNamee. All of a sudden I heard "fwoop fwoop fwoop". It was containers of napalm coming right down on us.

I knocked him down into an enemy foxhole. Several of my friends and people I knew were completely wiped out by the napalm, a lot of other people were burnt. We started firing green pop flares at them to let them know we were friendly. The jet pilots assumed that we were firing rockets at them. They couldn't see that because of how close they were to the ground and how fast they were going

Then they came back and bombed us with 250-pound bombs. Three landed in the ground about twenty feet from us and didn't go off.

But we were terrified that they were on time-release and might go off any moment. They then did three cannon-runs on us, and after that they went back to base.

RM: Even if you didn't happen to get your head blown off yourself, you had reason enough to be traumatized by what was going on around you.

PvA: On operations, I would like to add a few more stories before getting into that. Some operations would be sweep-and-burns where you would go and drag people out of their homes and burn their homes down to save them from Communism. [Ed. Note: known as the "Strategic Hamlet" program.] We would take them to new areas where supposedly there were building materials to build new houses and live under the South Vietnamese flag. After you dragged them out of their houses, burned them down, and dragged them across the country they weren't particularly happy. You got there and found out that the local government officials had sold all the building materials supplied by the US government for these people to the black market. There was nothing and they would just all sit on this hill on the ground with barbed wire around them.

These people would then sneak out and go back to their homes and rebuild. A plane would go over and drop pamphlets saying it was a "free-fire zone". At that point, we would go back and anything that moved, walked, talked, anything was shot. It was not considered alive anymore; you killed everything including water buffaloes. All justified because they had been warned that it was a free-fire zone. Having people do things like this is something that has been done in other wars. But people went over there thinking originally they were doing something good, in other words helping people against Communism. The Vietnamese people seemed to detest us. It turned out, you learned very quickly that this was not about anything but getting home alive. Friends were definitely dangerous to have.

RM: Why was that?

PvA: Because they would get you into trouble. I will go back now to Viet Nam quick and what happened, but I ended up going through several of these operations. On January 30th, 1967 I found tracks coming over the mountains and I estimated about 500 men.

I finally reported this after an argument with this corporal who had just come out from a supply company. He wouldn't believe that I knew what I was talking about until we followed them for a long time and the tracks went through the right type of underbrush where he could see that a lot of people had passed. We went back and reported it. We were told by our colonel, after the lieutenant reported it to them, for me to go out there.

He said "where do you think they are?"

I said "DengFu One".

He said, "Well take a patrol out there and see if they're there."

So the six of us went and I was correct and I was the only survivor of that. I was there for three and half hours alone. They would only give me six rounds of artillery because Hill 55 was low on it. They could have gotten to me in an hour and ten minutes but they took three and half hours. I wasn't particularly pleased. The corporal had his arm shot off and I wasn't sure if he was alive or dead. I was not happy being there, I had a tremendous amount of people trying to get me.

RM: I get completely wrapped up in the drama of the thirteen months you spent there and I know you have a story to tell as well about what happened in the years after you got back to the states under this broad heading of PTSD. Let's go to a time closer to now.

PvA: On January 13th, 1987 I was a heroin addict out of control in Phoenix, AZ. I finally became suicidal and was taken in by a fellow Viet Nam vet who insisted I come with him. He knew what I was going to do and took me to the VA hospital in Menlo Park, California. I was in the hospital for a year; I ended up in a psychiatric unit for PTSD. From there, my personal experience was not a good one in there, and I came out rather desperate. I serendipitously bumped into a gentleman who worked in PTSD. His name was Gerald French who was associated with a psychiatrist in Palo Alto by the name of Dr. Frank Gerbode. Gerbode had developed a technique that they felt would work very well in this area [of PTSD]. I was one of the first people to go through the technique. Not that it is a panacea for everything in life, but one thing that I've found is: the person I once thought I was, I now know I'm not.

RM: Pieter, I have the impression that for a number of years after the war you first of all didn't think you had a problem or denied you had a problem or got rotten help from the professional community for the problem.

PvA: At first, when I was told I had the problem I got furious because I was not a sissy. I found out it has nothing to do with being a sissy. Since being released from the VA hospital, I went to work with Dr. Gerbode and with Gerald French. They have a technique which is called Traumatic Incident Reduction (TIR). It is not psychology and it's not psychotherapy, in fact what it really is is an educational procedure.

The root of the word education has at its root "drawing out". You draw out what a person already knows.

In this procedure, you become aware of exactly what it is that is troubling you and you get to take a new look at what decisions you made or what you did not get complete looking at. It is non-evaluative and nobody is going to tell you that you are good or bad. Having somebody else tell you why you did it, how you felt, the reasons you're doing what you're doing, is absolutely ridiculous.

Unlike what happened to me before, once I had done this I no longer have a problem with these incidents affecting me in my present life. What we've found so far is that after fifteen to 40 hours of TIR, the PTSD symptoms are gone.

RM: Now give me a little rundown of the kind of symptoms you had going into this.

PvA: After I got back, I had a severe problem with being jumpy. I had a problem with being terrified of losing my temper. I couldn't walk in wooded areas (due to restimulation). I'm classified as having PTSD hypervigilance which means I'm always on the lookout for what's going on. I did a lot of private crying. I could always put on a macho front that everything was fine, but when I was alone I had a lot of trouble. Sometimes I would spend weeks holed up in my apartment and not want to go out. Eventually I would be forced to go out because of no food. That was something that seemed to get worse in the twenty years [at that time] since the war.

RM: This was not the condition you were in prior to the war. This was attributable to the experience there?

PvA: I had no idea that it had anything to do with it in any way. When I ended up suicidal, a psychiatrist in Phoenix just sat and listened. After two days and about four hours later, he told me that I had chronic PTSD. I didn't know what he meant. When he explained it to me I got furious because I was not a sissy. He basically left me alone and the staff gave me a booklet printed by the Disabled American Veterans (DAV) called "Symptoms and Etiology of PTSD".

RM: You had this in-patient experience in Phoenix with a psychiatrist who was the first after a considerable period of time to listen and understand what was going on, although you didn't immediately buy it?

PvA: This was my first experience with psychiatry; I had not sought help in twenty years. I did not know, I just thought that I was a bad guy. In 1982, I had some heroin and before I knew it, it was a great way not to deal with my problems. I became a heroin addict. It seemed to give one something to do so that one didn't have to deal with one's problems.

RM: I want to underscore the message that you don't have to have been shot, injured, or wounded in any way or have engaged in hot combat to have been thoroughly traumatized by what was going on around you. To have to live these post-war years using heroin, alcohol, or any kind of drug is the pits.

In closing, I've had an opportunity on this program over the last couple of years to talk to a lot of good people. I've had on my line guest psychiatrists and psychologists, authors of books, some of them very good, because I'm very selective. But when I heard of Dr. Gerbode's work in this area of traumatic stress reduction, I went to San Francisco and took an opportunity to get acquainted with it because it sounded good. I found out that it didn't just sound good, it was absolutely remarkable in its efficiency and its effectiveness. There isn't anything going on in the professional community among my colleagues in psychology or psychiatry or counseling or psychotherapy that is it's equal. I'm quite convinced that Dr. Gerbode's Traumatic Incident Reduction is the state-of-the-art handling for the post traumatic stress disorder and related disorders.

PvA: I've spent the last twenty years kindof thinking about stuff. The difference that I've experienced now is phenomenal. In fact, when I began doing TIR through Dr. Gerbode, my request was "to know what one hour of happiness was". Looking back on that, it either makes me cry or I don't believe I said it.

Martin H. Ray

16 The Face of the Enemy

My world, growing up, was much like your world, growing up, in that war was always present but at a distance. The Revolutionary War gave birth to our nation, the Civil War preserved the Union, the World Wars defended freedom and democracy in the Twentieth Century.

What I knew about war was fun and exciting. The Cavalry got the Indians, the Marines raised the flag at Iwo Jima, and George Washington rode a white horse. The most troubling image in my childhood occurred in the third episode of Disney's *Davy Crocket* where the hero and Jim Bowie were massacred at the Alamo.

In my mind, when I fought in a war, it would be quiet and bloodless and stealthy. I would pick off the enemy one by one at a hundred yards through a scope. I would swoop around supersonically firing magic missiles. I would be a frogman infiltrating beach barriers.

In my youth I liked to study history and geography. The United States was at the center of our world map. All the countries were represented in pastel colors with fixed outlines. Bad forces might try to change this picture, but good forces would hold it together. That was the bottom line of international relations. Change was the enemy.

I was born at the time of the Cold War. We and our allies were holding off the Communists. Just thinking about hordes of Russians and Chinese made me shiver. Russians were bear-like and dressed in furs. Chinese had slanted eyes and were sneaky. Russians and Chinese were the enemy.

While I was growing up, a little ember of the Cold War heated up in Viet Nam. Viet Nam is next to China. On my childhood map it was colored purple, a French colony, so it was in "our column". That was how I saw it. But then Vietnamese nationalists fought to expel the Japanese and French occupation forces during the 1940s and 50s. They won an election in 1956 to govern their country as communists. They took aid from our enemies the Russians and Chinese. We supported the non-communists in the South in a civil war, at first with advisors and equipment, eventually with half a million American troops. I was one of those.

I went to Viet Nam to face the enemy. I went to test my manhood. I went to taste war. Now four decades later, I want to report to you with pictures of my story, and how my view of war has changed. I am the fourth consecutive generation in my family with the name Martin H. Ray to serve my country in war. My great-grandfather earned this medal in the American Civil War. My grandfather's four sons all graduated from Service Academies and fought in World War II. Here are my Dad and Uncle Alan in the uniforms of West Point and Annapolis, with their father, sister, and youngest brother Roger. Uncle Roger joined my father in the invasion of Europe against Hitler. Here they are reunited with their father after both being wounded in the War and receiving the Purple Heart.

Uncle Martin the Third received the Purple Heart too, as well as the Navy Cross, the Navy's second highest medal. He died heroically helping to evacuate his men from their sinking ship torpedoed by the Japanese at the Battle of Midway. The Navy named this ship after him, the *USS Martin H. Ray*. My parents gave me his name too.

My father, an Army colonel, served 30 years in his career. During World War II he met my mother who was an Army Nurse in Europe. A few years later I was born at West Point, New York, where he taught military law. West Point is pictured in the lower left corner of this screen, alongside what my grandfather called "the majestic Hudson". We lived all over the United States, in Japan and Burma. You see a photograph of my sister and me at Fort Sill, Oklahoma, where my father took artillery training. My own first experience in uniform was in the Boy Scouts where I earned the Eagle Scout Award.

When I entered college in 1964 at Johns Hopkins University I joined the ROTC program. You can see that ROTC was a natural course for me. I believed that everyone should give a period of service to his country, in some way. Mine would be in the Army. The Army gave me a scholarship to college.

While in school I competed on the intercollegiate rifle team and was elected captain of the team my senior year. It was the beginning of my familiarity with weapons on target ranges. I loved making a tight pattern of bullet holes in the center of the target. I learned how to be focused, how to breathe, ice in the veins, caressing the trigger exactly. I learned how to balance tension and relaxation, inhaling, exhaling, sweeping the rifle barrel through just the right arc to a momentary rest, BANG, a bullet on its way home to raise our score. I earned this Rifle Team Medal to wear on my uniform, and a varsity letter to wear on my school sweater.

Between the junior and senior years we cadets went off to ROTC summer camp at Indiantown Gap, Pennsylvania. There the paper targets morphed from bull's-eyes to human silhouettes. We simulated the deadly business of battle with hand-to-hand combat, bayonet training, thrust and parry, stabbing straw dummies yelling *KILL! KILL! KILL!* We qualified with pistols, machine guns, grenades. We handled the new M-16 rifle on the Quick-Kill course, shooting reflexively from the hip at pop-up targets. In the jungle, death lurked only a few feet and a fraction of a second away with no time to aim. I earned the Expert Marksmanship Badge to wear on my uniform. We came back to the serenity of our final year in the classroom.

College graduation brought my Regular Army commissioning as a second lieutenant in June of 1968. I studied for six more weeks at the Engineer Officer's Basic Course in Fort Belvoir, Virginia. Then I took three months of the Army's toughest training at Fort Benning, Georgia. Airborne School prepared us to parachute behind enemy lines to destroy them with the element of surprise. Ranger School developed the stamina and skills of commando unit leaders. I was welcomed into the Army's elite fighters. I earned the privilege of wearing Airborne Wings on my chest, and the Ranger Tab on my sleeve above any unit insignia.

Military training is the ultimate sport. We learned our skills, we learned our roles, and primarily we learned to work as a team. We learned to extend our abilities and our limits far beyond what we had thought possible. In the classroom and in the field we exposed ourselves to the meaning of courage and exhaustion and the necessity of making life-and-death decisions in chaotic conditions. The Army threw every challenge they could think of to take us to the breaking point in the game, to simulate the test of battle. But we were still schoolboys. Until blood flowed, until we wasted our opponents, until our mates got mangled, until any breath might be our last, it was still a game. We hadn't yet hunted to the death other human beings, and been hunted by them in return. What we lacked in training camp was a real enemy to hate.

I entered the Army with a four-year service obligation in the Corps of Engineers. I planned to see the world. I wanted a stint of outdoor construction work after all those years in the classroom. The Viet Nam War was going on but it seemed remote to me during my first two assignments to construction units in Thailand and Germany. I wanted to build up rank and experience before going to war. We heard that second lieutenant platoon leaders had the shortest life span of anyone on the battlefield.

In June of 1971 it was time for the final year of my contract—a transfer to Viet Nam. By now I had attained the rank of captain, eligible to be a company commander of perhaps 120 men in three or four platoons each led by a lieutenant. After some home leave and a visit to my college roommate in British Columbia, I boarded a plane in Seattle for the flight over. We landed at Cam Ranh Bay. The plane taxied to a sandbagged shelter guarded by barbed wire and machine gunners. Things were getting serious. We went inside the replacement depot where the Army would match us up with its manpower needs. We would be taking the places of men who had been killed or wounded, or who had rotated home after finishing their tours of duty.

Being Airborne/Ranger qualified I applied for a position with the 101st Airborne Division combat engineers who were then fighting near the DMZ, the de-militarized zone at the border with North Viet Nam. I wanted to be with the sharpest troops in the country, even if they were in the thick of things. Oddly enough, I was sent to Saigon to a desk job at the Combined Intelligence Center. For the next year I helped prepare terrain studies for units who were slugging it out in the field, but I was stationed in a completely different world from them.

During my daily commute to work I passed through parts of the City bustling with vendors and schoolchildren. In colonial times Saigon had been called 'The Paris of the East'. Now it was choked with refugees forced from the countryside. Everybody was trying to make a little life for himself and his family. Here you see two young women downtown wearing silk *ao dais*, traditional Vietnamese dresses that float elegantly in the tropical heat. Around the capital city we witnessed the cost of war only indirectly, such as when my office sponsored a Christmas party at an orphanage for children whose families had been killed in the fighting.

Each of us soldiers on the staff drew a weapon for emergencies. We were supposed to practice with it, and keep it in good shape. But the war seemed far away. Mingling with the Vietnamese struck me as both exotic and perfectly normal. I went to homes, markets, temples, and a wedding. The groom, a pilot in the South Vietnamese Air Force, married his sweetheart as departing combatants have always done. While the family gathered for portraits we all felt the war in the background. The bride received a sadly reassuring hug from her mother.

I began to see that weapons were no longer a sport. Their real purpose began to give me a horrible feeling. Despite my years of marksmanship training, I sensed how repulsive it would be to use them against people. I'll never forget the first night I reported for security duty at the headquarters. Part of my job involved checking stations around the building, armed with a .45 caliber pistol. I stared at that pistol and didn't see how I could shoot somebody with it in the event of an encounter. My hands shook. I looked down at them as though they had a separate existence from me. They refused to cooperate with loading the bullets into the gun. When the briefing officer wasn't looking I threw the ammunition clip back into the drawer, strapped on the empty pistol and went out on my rounds. I never loaded that gun all year. I was fortunate to be far from the front lines where the killing was taking place.

One day I signed up for a course in photography at the Saigon Education Center. This opened up a new world for my free time in the evenings. I began to see interesting scenes in the street, like these food vendors by a movie poster. My class went out to a village on a field trip to take pictures. We passed by farmers working in rice paddies. Back in the darkroom I developed the negatives and prepared to make my first prints. I'll never forget the moment those images appeared in the developing tray. The faces of Viet Nam came into focus with universal beauty.

At every opportunity I explored Saigon in search of its human story. I took buses downtown, meandered through streets, markets, temples and parks, taking pictures everywhere. Printing them in the isolation of the darkroom always amazed me. The noise, the dust, the heat and smells of the background disappeared. With the camera's selective lens I entered a world where the burden of the war disappeared. In the faces, through the photographs, I saw the hopes and dreams of people everywhere.

During my tour the US government became increasingly frustrated with the bloody stalemate in the Viet Nam War. Over 50,000 Americans and millions of Vietnamese had died without meeting our goal of preventing the unification of the country under a Communist regime. The American people became tired of the casualties and the expense and the failure to achieve victory in a faraway land. Our military reduced its ground troops and stepped up the bombing. Any place we suspected of enemy occupation we pulverized from the air. Our planes saturated Viet Nam with four times the explosives that the American and British Air Forces dropped on Germany during World War II. The enemy wouldn't quit.

American troops were engaged in guerrilla warfare with indefinite battlefronts. The enemy was able to blend into the population and the countryside. We struggled to identify who and where they were. Since we couldn't see them my Area Analysis Section was asked to help draw up bombing targets on the basis of geographic probabilities. We outlined maps with likely hiding places. Sometimes the Air Force would try to confirm activity by sprinkling the designated areas with little parachute-dropped sensors, which could detect and radio back movements and sounds and even smells. The idea was to improve our chances of hitting somebody in the jungle.

One afternoon I received an urgent order to develop targeting information by early the next day. I kept my team up working all night to prepare the recommendations, and was asked to brief a general early in the morning. I went down the hall to deliver our results in the conference room. At the conclusion the general put his hand on my shoulder and said "Well done, Captain", while my boss looked on. I felt swell. At the end of my year in country I was awarded the Joint Services Commendation Medal by America and the Staff Service Medal First Class by the Republic of Vietnam.

But that particular morning, as I walked back down the hall from the briefing room, my thoughts became cloudy. I wondered if the B-52s were on the way to waste those circles we had drawn on the map. We called the bombing strikes Arc Lights, or Rolling Thunder. We used a picture of such an airstrike on Chieu Hoi leaflets to convince enemy sympathizers to switch sides. I knew that I didn't have any clear idea of whom those bombs would fall on in the countryside that day, but I had diligently led my team to choose the targets for the sake of a pat on the back. I felt unclean.

I began to wonder what caused my country to intervene militarily in Viet Nam, to have to kill an enemy there. I wondered why I liked the medals so much. At least two million Vietnamese people like the ones in my photographs died in the tragedy. There were many points of view. At one extreme was the man who told me that we weren't prosecuting the war forcefully enough. He advocated using nuclear weapons to destroy North Vietnamese cities, one by one, until they quit. "What about the inhabitants?" I asked. "Incinerate them!" he replied.

David Bianchini

17

Letter to Shane

[Ed. Note: in general, we have tried to preserve this document in its original state.]

SHANE...

Well... Well... Well... It's about bloody fuckin' time... you say... Yes sir... I know... I've been bloody bad about this letter writing business... but alas... comrade... here I am... in all my wordy psychotic abandon... back to pummeling you with my do-da-day... from this kindergarten... so... let me see... what about frolicking in the fumes of the frantic... yeah... that should do it... okey... are your ready... no... we won't be needin that life preserver... are you ready... no flack jacket here... too much weight... would slow us down... got to be able to move fast... no place for the timid... hear me boy... yeah... that's it... let's just jump in... let go... let's just DO IT...

"DON'T MEAN NOTHING... DON'T MEAN A THING"... Ricocheted squealing... flaming frolic... jungle rot and joviality... magical mayhem... medal monkeys... wheezing chest wounds... violated... amputated... royally bitched forever... marshmallow faces... quadraplegics... splenectomies... teen age colostomies... nothin left to diddle... swabbin blood... changing dressings... bouncing Betty's... eighteen year-old stumpers... flying fleshettes... trache tubes... dopamine... compresses for crispy critters... IV bags full of glucose and morphine... Willie-peter... Napalm... Depersonalize Davey Boy... "IT DON'T MEAN NOTHIN... DON'T MEAN A THING"... multiple frag wounds... body bags... give him a cap to the noodle... punji "shit" sticks... C-4... gasses... flames... herbicided forests... burning earth... poisoned rice paddies... withering heat... curled up life... splintering smoking earth... M-16s... M-60s... M-79s... 155s ... 105s... B-52s... 750 pounders... and cripples... cripples... cripples... so many missing parts... arms, hands... fingers... ears... feet... crutches... waddling stumps... fingerless hands begging... droves of exquisite deformed beings... Yes, Sir... RE... Yippee for genocide... sure has an intimate face don't it, Davey Boy... the goody-goody soup of human bone... gristle... tissue and feces... sip up the bag... 1st class ticket home... 21-gun salute... all in the name of duty...

in the service of murder and mayhem... pious homilies... patriotic claptrap... saccharine bullshit... stuffed severed privates... agent orange... white phosphorous... chinooks... Hueys... puff the magic dragon... RPGs... Indian country... cobras... B-40 rockets... frags... LZ... Miniguns... mission support sites... concertina (Turner) wire... starlight scopes... people sniffers... butterfly bombs... trip flares... spookys... KA-BAR knife... AK47s... water torture... Bell telephone hour... electrocutions... ambushes... assassinations... hosings... killings... mutilating... masturbating DEATH... free-fire zone... ""Rub Em Out"... "waste Em"... "Cap Em"... terracide... Human carrion... puddles of pumping agony... infected zip quiff... chopped and buggered... threaded ears... entrails... spleens... livers... kidneys... YUM... YUM... HUMAN COTTON CANDY... lick those chops... Yes, sir... Davey Boy... Yippie... Stump City... Old civilization is beginning to have a tart taste... ain't it, Davey Boy... "DON'T mean nothin... it don't MEAN A THING"... BLOOD... maggots... decaying brains... eyes puffed out... shut... bloated corpses... swollen lips... pink fat tongues... leg akimbo... flies feasting on rotting peckers in surrender... OH YEAH... my man Ho... THE DEVIL... THAT LITTLE BASTARD MADE ME DO IT... HONEST... AFTER ALL... GOT TO BE A REASON... GOT TO HAVE AN ANSWER... AN EXCUSE... SOME RATIONAL... TO PERISH ALL THOSE LITTLE FUCKERS... CAN'T JUST SAY WHOOPS, SORRY... didn't mean to turn your world topsy-turvy... sorry I sent you and your family to bloody fuckin HELL... Yes, Sir... just like snappin your fingers... Slam Bam, Thank you Ma'am... SEE Ya... wouldn't want to be ya... and It all seems like a fuckin fairy tale to the ones you tell... Cinderella with a scythe... Yes, Sir... like all those bodies are nothin but a moldy fuckin shag rug... after all... my boy... you gots to smell... taste a place like Scat-Man-Do... Fire Base Sweat Pea... The Fish Hook... Parrot's Beak... No, Sir... this ain't no guessing-game... no fuckin ring toss here... sure did get your teeth kicked down your throat by those little bastards in The Fish Hook... didn't you, Davey Boy... those slant eyed, rice eating-ruck-humping mothers hawked a good glop of phlegm and spit right in your face at Scat Man Do... didn't they, Davey Boy... ""WHIP IT ON ME YOU FUCKIN SLOPEHEADS... YOU SAID... DIDN'T YOU, DAVEY BOY... AND DID THEY EVER... MY BOY... REALLY LAID IT ON YOU THICK AND HEAVY LIKE... GREASED HALF YOUR TEAM BEFORE YOU SAY... "PUT UP OR SHUT UP... DIDN"T THEY, DAVEY BOY...

Yes, Sir... Davey Boy... It's about fuckin time you picked yourself up off the ground... brushed yourself off of all this firefight jungle funk... Right as Rain... those ears around your neck ain't no cheerleader's Pom-Pom... besides... the game's over... you don't need no bone-numbing booney-voodoo to ward off that jungle boogy-man no more... everything's hunky-dory... no incoming tonight... no slant-eyed banditoes be tappin on your shoulder tonight... And now you're really layin back in your web... aren't you, my boy... really savorin the juices... lovin it... really lickin your fingers... really got yourself in a trance... really can hear the echoes... the breathless sweating out of your boony-backtrack dreams... Ain't nothing to rely on... nobody to hang onto... no way, my man... you got to do this baby by your lonesome... no buddy-buddy... your innards... no passengers... you got to do it from were you's a-sittin... and that's that... got to just DO IT... no... you ain't got nobody to Jack you when you is a-crashin... nobody to slam that fucker to the elbow when grittin your teeth don't work no more... that devil... He's livin on the edge of your heart... from here on out... and that's that... You FALLA... so, Davey Boy... don't get used to nothin... besides... nobody can deal with your jungle junk for long... you know that... besides... that devil... he sure leaves an enticing scent toward that inferno... don't he... yeah... Davey... you sure do like that smell, don't you my boy... What's it smell like, my boy... Mennen Skin Bracer... french fries... burning tires... scorched flesh... wakes you right up... pulls you like a fuckin magnet... don't it, my boy... Can't help yourself, can you my boy... well... nobody else can either, my boy... at least not for long... no sense gettin sentimental about it, my boy... No, Sir... not from where you're sittin... No, Sir... you can't afford any mush from where you're at... it'll squash you like a bug... can't afford no luxuries from the crate you're sittin on... can't deal with such diddly from there... Oh Hell, Man... just remember... when all that BLEEDING... STABBING... THROBBING... EXPLODING... BOONY BACKRACK SHIT CRACKS YOU... WHEN YOU'RE ALL ALONE IN THE MIDDLE OF THE NIGHT LAYING ON YOUR RACK... LIKE THE END OF A WET TOWEL IN A LOCKER ROOM FIGHT... IT DON'T MEAN NOTHING... DON'T MEAN A THING...

Sooooooo, GOOD Buddy... How the devil are you... been away for a while... been in the hole for a month... it's good to get AWAY from the buzz of everyday life every once in a while... as you of all people know so well... Back to painting... it's going better than expected... I've been documenting this place and my experiences... sort of TRANSFERING my anti-social obsessive compulsive behavior from one agenda to another... perhaps a show someday... I'm sending all my stuff to New

York... where it is being framed... and compiled... me and John Wayne Gacy... or perhaps I've got to kill a gross of teenagers before I'm able to show my work with any success...

I was reading the Newspaper the other day... It seems as though there is this toad in Arizona, the Bufo alvarius... better known as the Colorado River Toad... It secretes a milky-white substance that is a psychoactive drug under Arizona Law... People have been licking them... getting arrested... the police have been setting traps... hiding behind bushes and leaping out just in time to catch the dirty little toad-lickers in the act... I used to get high when I licked pussy... Can you imagine the charges and sentences once the government realizes the state of arousal pussy-licking creates... both for the giver AND RE-CEIVER... What do you suppose the statute of limitations on pussy-licking will be... It's been about three years now...but I've done enough pussy-licking to get the electric chair seven or eight times...

How about Woodstock... I missed it again... Were you at the first one... Yeah, you were too young... who knows... maybe your parents took you... anyway... this one sounded like a fucking police-state... Dogs sniffing... metal detectors... DEA agents arresting every Deadhead they could find... In the '69 Woodstock Abbie Hoffman got slammed in the back by Pete Townsend's guitar and pushed off the stage... while he was ranting and raving... When Hoffman was asked about the incident years later just before he committed suicide... he said "If this is such a big fuckin incident... Where's the goddamn picture?"... as if our reality is conferred by the camera...the media... the slogans... and not our eyes... our experiences... or memories... Oh well... the fuckin war between IMAGE and REALITY... goes on... time's almost up with this typewriter... and I gotta be moseyin' outta town... You sound like you are doing great... I don't say this to many people... but... You have profound talents, my friend... flashing brilliance... in that coco-loco cranium of yours... and the fury and fire to go along with it... very rare today... most people live their lives as the carpenter... whose work goes so slowly for the dullness of his tools that he has not the time to sharpen them... all I can say... is... keep up your artistic aims... in the end it is the only thing that will lend some sanity... some healthy clarity to that virulent virus called MAN...

Miss you more than a cheeseburger on an onion roll... red onion... and brown mustard... more than Ham and Swiss on pumpernickel bread... more than lean roast beef on a kaiser roll (hey... Kaiser's a good name for a kid)... with horseradish... more than a morning piss even...

Monsieur, Don Juan, Bark, Baklava, Bhagavad Gita, Henry Blanton the last cowboy, John Wilkes Booth, Ban Chennedy...

I'm doing a portrait of you... but you ain't going to get it... unless of course you are the highest bidder at the Sotheby's auction.

This letter was written while the author was serving 180 days in solitary confinement at the Fairton Correctional Facility, New Jersey in the Spring of 1997.

Tom Skiens

18   Boat People

Charlie Company, 4th Battalion 3d Infantry Regiment, 11th Light infantry Brigade, American Division

I will attempt to maintain the integrity of this story but I will not name names for those who issued or executed orders to kill. It would serve no purpose to identify them now.

Depending on your religion this particular day, or moment and your ideology lost, revived or rebuilding, the following story could be considered murder or as one person said, "There is no murder in war." This story must certainly be about a killing, the ending of life. I know in some small way, my life ended during the week leading up to this event.

Please understand that I am just a grunt, but I believe this week was dominated by a single ill-conceived objective. The objective was to cordon off an area of sniper-alley, drop CS gas from the 4.2 mortars inside the cordoned area and shoot the sniper as he ran away from the CS gas. This was a great plan designed by great men. Except that gas goes up when you release it because it's lighter than air. The gook sniper was living in a hole in the ground. We had a snowball's chance in hell of pulling this mission off successfully.

I think the frustration and losses we suffered during this mission help define us as a combat infantry unit. Elements of Charlie Company became cynical, mean, without reason. They would kill for a shot of adrenaline or because they could. They would rape to hide their fears or because they wanted to.

It was during this terrible week of April 1968 where we hit seven booby traps, suffered one wounded from a sniper, thirteen wounded overall and six dead. Hargrove and Pennimon died from a Bouncing Betty; the LT lost his right foot, and fingers off the right hand; an FNG, who had just arrived at about 1900 on the resupply chopper the night before, was wounded in the gut.

Zimmerman and I were right in the middle of the mess. We were both also right in the middle of the January 13, 1968 Bouncing Betty that killed two and wounded eight. Zimmerman and I do not know each other at that time, but we kept showing up at the same mass-casualty events. Zimmerman still does not know me and I know him only indirectly through staff journals and a weird connection where Zimmerman is one of only two names I could remember when I came home from Nam. That's because he and another grunt would be dusted off April 25th as psycho cases. Zimmerman being the only original surviving member of Charlie Company, 1st Squad, 1st Platoon. Twice in four months, everyone else in the squad had become dead or wounded. I have always wanted to find Zimmerman and tell him I was proud of him for being the first to know when he had enough of war. The rest of us got traumatized but kept on trucking.

Two days later Sgt Fox is moving from left to right to get his point oriented when he was shot by a sniper. I crawled over and started using my radio to get help while Zimmerman retrieved all available information from Sgt Fox that would enable him to run the platoon. Zimmerman was a PFC but as things would have it he was the highest ranking person in the platoon. About one hour later Charlie Company hit another booby trap. More people down. I'm resigned, this shit will never stop.

So this is kind of what is going on this week. We are completing our mission but taking heavy losses. Heavy to me anyway. Sometime here we established an RON (Remain Over Night). We begin digging foxholes and opening C-rations. I always got rid of my blouse as it was heavy with sweat by 1000 and it was now around 1800.

Someone over near the river alerted us to two gooks in a sampan. I grabbed my M-16 and joined five or six others at the river's edge to have a look. The ranking member of the group said, "Hail the gooks and see if we get a response."

Someone said, "Lie Di, motherfucker."

Someone else said, "La Dia, motherfucker." We did not speak good or consistent gook.

The boss told the M-60 gunner to put warning rounds in the water. M-60 gunners love to fire their weapons. Each round fired is that much less weight to carry. The M-60 gunner let loose several bursts to let the gooks know we were talking to them. The gooks were waving their arms and repeating, "Me no VC, me no VC!" The boss let the M-60 gunner know they had followed the rules and it was now OK to shoot to kill.

Grunts get their buddies blown up every day. Grunts who could get blown up themselves and never get a chance to shoot back because Charlie is inviolable. These grunts were now told by authority that they could kill.

It did not take long for the M-60 gunner to depress and hold the trigger. 7.62 mm rounds spit up geysers of water as they plowed their way to the sampan. The M-60 kept up a heavy pace chewing up the water, then the boat, then the people. I watched the upright bodies, who most surely were dead, do the "spastic jerk-dance" and emit pieces of their bone and skin out the back of their body. The spastic jerk-dance is not done by those who are dead, but the energy imparted by rounds from opposing weapons keeps their bodies upright and in motion.

The boat started sinking and the bodies began slipping underwater. The order was issued to recover personnel and items from the narrow but deep river. The ammo-bearer for the M-60 jumped into the water. He quickly grabbed a dead gook and started moving it to the water's edge where two sets of ready hands began lifting the gook up the steep, muddy and very slick riverbank.

The grunt in the water paddled over to the second gook and repeated his motions. He then turned his focus to the floating debris and the need to secure the boat. The boss said "Forget about the boat and collect whatever documents you can." When he returned to the shore, everyone gave a hand helping the ammo-bearer out of the water.

We now search the bodies. That's what war is. A whole lot of searching bodies. It makes no difference whether the body is alive or dead. You may have lived in this place for 60 years and I may have just arrived 30 days ago, but I am going to search you. That's just the way it is. When your most trusted and loved buddy turns a prisoner over to you, you search the prisoner. Nothing else is acceptable.

You must search the prisoner before you turn it over to a buddy and he searches the prisoner before accepting it. There are no exceptions. You search everything all the time.

The search turned up two ID cards, American issue. One for each body. This was not the ideal situation we had hoped for. It would be nice if they would have had gook cards with big red stars, but they didn't. It would have been nice to find sores on their shoulders from carrying a backpack or rings in their toes or a bone in the nose, or something, but we didn't. These guys could very well have earned the American ID cards they were packing. When we reported this incident to higher-higher we said, "Engaged two VC, 2 VC KIA, sampan destroyed, no weapons."

It is hard for me to put this in the category of murder. It was certainly a killing. Unlawful acts occurred, but under orders. It had been a tough week. We had suffered a lot of casualties and blowing these guys away sort of took off some of the tension. Pretty lame excuse.

Killing because we are tired of others killing those around us. This was a revenge killing. Not that these two people in the boat had done anything to us personally, but simply because we needed to kill someone to help us feel like we could even the score. Killing to gain a sense of control over our lives. We did not win the war that day.

19 Off the Road

It was not a pilgrimage, not something planned and plotted grid by grid, though events turned out somewhat differently. In '95, having backpacked through Singapore, Thailand and Laos I flew from Vientiane to Hanoi, traveled down the coast, caught a motorcycle to Saigon's Long-Distance Bus Station. The ride to An Loc cost sixty cents and took ninety minutes. There were no foreigners. Only Vietnamese. Where would I stay? Who and what would I meet? And what of Quan Loi? These were magnetic questions.

When the bus lurched to a grinding halt in An Loc's neatly tiled center I grabbed my gear and jumped off; immediately a crowd gathered about the thin, weary tourist. A gaunt, soft-spoken man who later became my guide led me to the ramshackle Binh Long Hotel.

"Here OK," said Than. "Other place expensive."

Cramped and stuffy, my two-dollar-a-night room had a single hard mattress, torn mosquito netting, a solitary wood-hatched window. At night the heat was unbearable. Mornings, the Binh Long's communal bathroom was packed with noisy transient Asian men. The Chinese-style squat-latrines were not pleasant.

The following day Than and I rode his battered Honda Cub bike to Quan Loi. I hoped to find bunkers, gun pits, culvert hooches, the rubber trees which brought us merciful shade and where I first saw combat. After a breezy twenty minutes Than pulled over and parked the feisty scooter.

"Why are we stopping?"

My heart dropped when Than said, "We are here."

In fact, Quan Loi is gone, flat as field, the tarmac air strip scattered by phantom hands. The rest is bush and scrub and unforgettably red. The pummeling heat was unbearable. I poked around, plucked out an AK-47 cartridge, rusted and brittle, from the hard dry dirt. I took photographs: The remains of the strip, a wide-open field where the base once stood, a group of peasants planting corn. The ghosts of their dead filled their faces.

D 1/7 Cav, 3rd Platoon, LZ Compton (1969)

A sad, weather-beaten man wearing a tattered American Army shirt who spoke English said he was fifty-five years old; he appeared seventy. He said that during the war he had worked with the First Cavalry Division. I asked him if he could locate LZ Compton.

"Yes," he replied, pointing North, then pulled out his pockets, which were empty and flat, like elephant ears. "With the Americans I had money and food. I had my own house. Now I have nothing."

I turned to hide my face, then pressed fifty thousand dong, about two weeks' salary, into his hands. A few minutes later, through Than, I asked a colorfully dressed woman where she lived. She cautiously raised her arm and pointed Southeast. Than said the village was two miles away. All the peasants, young and old, wore sandals ground down beyond repair.

Than said that at war's-end scavengers and resettled peasants stripped the base; scrap metal was carted away, heavy weaponry stolen, homes were built from American timber. For years unexploded ordnance posed a constant danger; only recently has it been cleaned up. Still, Viet Nam is littered with live mortar and artillery shells, rotting, fragile 40 mm grenades, five hundred pound bombs, Agent Orange; even now all take their toll.

It was hot, the noon sun beat straight down. Than said he wanted to show me Lake Xosim. I said goodbye to the peasants, to Quan Loi, and hopped on his scooter.

"I think you will like," said Than.

The Cub raced forward over the good American blacktop. In minutes, the hot rushing air dried our sopping wet clothes.

The sleepy village around the lake lay untouched by time. Small neat houses with terracotta roofs encircled the clear and tranquil waters; low brambled coffee plants edged the lake perimeter. Exquisite open air pagodas with graceful walkways served as landing docks; I watched a fisherman grip and sway and cast his net. Two hundred meters out, at the lake's center, a sun-bleached bamboo platform, ghostlike and skeletal, stood eerily at rest. Than said no one swam here anymore. Too many people had drowned after holiday drinking. Their spirits haunted the water.

"I want to show you something else," he said.

We walked a short way through partially cleared jungle. The remains of an old French fort, built completely of stone, rose up heavy and hypnotic. The laughter of children playing badminton echoed off the moss-covered stones. Than looked at me, but I could not speak.

That evening I met Ba, manager at the Binh Long hotel. Short, trim and pleasant, like Than, he too had worked for the Americans. Both had spent hard time in re-education camps. Both studiously avoided this topic.

"What is the English word for big machines that push earth?" Ba asked.

I closed my eyes a moment, scanning a distant landscape. "Bulldozers?"

Ba nodded grimly. "We put bodies in a big hole after fighting."

Some say the 1972 Battle of An Loc was the greatest battle of the war. At the time I knew nothing of it.

Late at night on the third day I had unexpected visitors.

"Wake up! Wake up!" said Ba, repeatedly knocking on the hard wood door. "The police are here. They wish to speak with you."

"I'm sleeping," I said. "Tell them to go away. I'll talk to them tomorrow."

My travels in Third World countries had taught me not to be intimidated. Still, what could they want?

On the first day, I had handed a copy of my passport (never once giving the real item at any guesthouse) to the hotel clerk. However few foreigners visited An Loc and she had put it aside. Informed of my presence, the police tracked me down.

"You come out. You please talk with them," Ba demanded. Given the urgent tone in his voice I quickly dressed, and unlocked the door. In the narrow hallway, two thin officers, identical in black caps and light green uniforms pressed a litany of questions.

"Where is your passport? How long do you stay? Do you have drugs? Do you have camera? Where will you travel in An Loc?"

Viet Nam was and remains a secretive culture. Ba, standing erect and humble, dutifully translated. After ten minutes I agreed to visit police headquarters.

At dawn, the air sweet and cool, Than and I drove past thick, impenetrable jungle, past infinite rows of stately rubber trees, at last arriving at a squat one-storey building on the town's outskirts. Inside a damp, musty ill-lit room several American carbines hugged a mildewed wall. Their battered wood stocks embraced once gleaming gunmetal now dull and pitted. A policeman pointed to a school-child's seat. For nearly an hour, I filled out tissue-thin forms in triplicate.

Later that day, riding a borrowed bike, I returned to the haunting rows of symmetrical rubber, strung my GI hammock between two slender trees and slept while mosquitoes hummed and bit. Waking, covered with itching welts, I rode back and chatted with Than and his family. At 9 pm his wife and young daughter went to bed. For hours, as a light rain tapped on the roof, Than and I talked of war. Many things were said in silence.

The following day, by a sad stroke of luck I stumbled upon the town hospital. In 1972, 10,000 civilians and combatants had died in three months of fighting. I walked the hospital grounds, stared in awe at split-open buildings, the walls pocked by bullets and skittering shrapnel. I drew diagrams, inspected dark, abandoned med/surg wards untouched by time. A wary female doctor spoke of scarce medical equipment, types of patients treated, glanced at a woman who lay dying on an American gurney. "Suicide by poison," she said, which might have been true.

At night, I heard enormous trucks rumble through town from ten till dawn. Ba said these were timber convoys hauling wood illegally cut in Cambodia. Trundling past, each trailer lugged 50 immense logs held fast by heavy link chains. Hurried red numbers were chalked over the stiff dead trunks; they could have been bodies.

Four days later I stood outside the Binh Long Hotel, waiting to leave An Loc. When the bus arrived, Than and I embraced. Much was said in those moments. I've written him several times and received replies, though money sent went missing.

"First Loc Ninh, then Bu Dop," I said, waving farewell.

The bus to Loc Ninh cost 30 cents and took 25 minutes. It was here the Americans fought NVA troops funneled down the legendary Ho Chi Minh trail. Past the grim town center I took a room in a shabby concrete hotel. An English-speaking man with a motorcycle offered to be my guide. He said only MIA teams had visited An Loc. An hour later the police ordered me out.

"I'm cold and tired, it's late, I don't drive, I have a room, I haven't eaten, I need sleep, and no, you can't have my passport," I said to three sergeants, two lieutenants and finally a stone-faced major. Ten years earlier this sort of talk risked jail or expulsion. I was both stupid and lucky.

"What do you know about war?" the major snarled.

"I fought here," I said. "I'm looking for LZ Compton. An American firebase."

Where I watched a man's brains spill onto brick-red mud as medic's dragged him away.

"Get out. You must leave now," said the major.

My guide, translating, gave me an anxious look. Unlike him, I felt strong and confident facing this enemy.

"Alright," I said. "But I'll leave tomorrow."

"Give me your passport," the major growled.

"No. I'll give you a copy." Tucked beneath my shirt, I opened my money belt. Plucked out a paper square. Handed it to him. "Here," I snapped. "Keep it."

I walked away, unaware that during the furious Easter Tide offensive, American B-52s, thousands of North Vietnamese with tanks and artillery, fought a pitched battle against American backed ARVN. The town was pulverized. Some say Loc Ninh has yet to recover.

A long ugly scar stitched across her face, "Me hit by rocket," said the owner of the cement hotel, smiling as she pointed to her indented frontal lobe. "My daughter hit by rocket. My daughter five years. My daughter dead."

An unspeakable demon-grin filled her childlike face. I ate supper, lay down, tossed and turned in my cavernous room, rose early, and caught the first bus out.

"Here, I want to go here," I would tell drivers, pedestrians, street vendors, anyone who would listen, pointing to Song Be province on a glossy 50-cent map bought in Saigon. "I'm trying to find LZ Compton."

After the third time in two days heading to the wrong town on National Highway 13, I hollered, "Stop!" The peasants on the sweltering bus giggled when I jumped off. Sometimes traveling makes you crazy. Jungle edging both sides of the road, I threw down my pack, sat on it, and wept. A minute later a crowd of well-mannered children surrounded me.

"Where-are-you-from? What-is-your-name? How-old-you-are?", they sweetly badgered.

I sat silent as stone until all had departed. All save for a dear child who pedaled her blue bike in tight, uniform circles, and in perfect English asked, "What do you want, Sir? My father can help you. Please, Sir. Where do you want to go?"

As if she were the adult I lamented, "Go away. I don't need anything. Just go away."

I hitched, got lost, snared a ride at a check point from a fat, slick haired cop.

"You-wait-here," he said, then returned, gripping the handlebars of 1500cc Kawasaki. I hopped on, threw my arms around his ample waist, (careful to avoid the holstered US Army .38 caliber pistol) as we sped 50 miles an hour to the same wrong town.

"This Song Be," he said, his right fist sweeping the air. A welcoming billboard read, 'Tu Dao Mot.' I smiled. He zoomed off, a puff of blue smoke trailing behind the engines loud roar. The search for LZ Compton had ended.

I hoisted my pack and trudged to a nearby restaurant. Once seated, the cheerful waitress, a former American employee, introduced her supervisor, an elder woman with a slender build.

"She NVA. In war, she shoot me," she said.

The supervisor cocked her hand, pistol-like, and put it to her subordinate's head.

"Now we friend," the waitress tittered.

The happy pair watched me pluck stale noodles from a chipped ceramic bowl. The thin gruel was tasteless. A full plate of fruit salad was superb.

Refreshed, I walked down a wide black road dotted with flimsy shops and spindly trees which stood scourged and withered. Dark heavy clouds loomed overhead. I spotted a corrugated metal porch roof a hundred meters away. The sky turned coal black, streaks of lightning snapped across the horizon. I walked as fast as I could. Then it began to rain.

None too soon, I huddled beneath the roof; a moment later the wooden door creaked open. Nguyen, short and wiry, invited me inside his neat, cozy house. He introduced me to his wife, a shy thin woman who smiled diminutively. He flicked on the light of a large aquarium. A huge goldfish swam indifferently back and forth. Nguyen reached into a bookcase, selected a volume, proudly opened his BMW manual.

"Before war I work in Germany," he said, holding the book like a bible. Outside, sheets of rain swept over the roof; torrents swamped the street. Closing the book, Nguyen said, "Soon, we look for hotel."

When the rain stopped Nguyen disappeared into a small room, then wheeled out a shiny Honda Cub. His wife opened the front door. "Good meeting," she said. We touched palms. On the porch, Ngyuen mounted the bike, inserted a key, and began the ritual of kickstarting. On the fourth try, a throaty roar and lush black plume announced success. I hopped on behind him. Off we sped, the wheels cutting a path through flooded alleys and nameless streets, until we suddenly arrived at a bland, dismal building which appeared empty. My hopes skyrocketed.

Nguyen switched off the motor. "I wait," he said.

Inside, a young gaunt-faced clerk wearing wire-rim spectacles said, "Passport..." Reluctantly, I handed the prized document to him. His gaze fastened on the gold-stamped American eagle, one talon clutching an olive branch, the other a cluster of thirteen arrows. He looked at me full in the face, wagged a finger in the air. "No foreigner allowed," he said. Then muttered, "Sorry."

Nguyen patted the back of his seat. "I show you more," he said.

We drove to a monolithic five-storey building whose drab cement blocks alternated with large rectangular windows. A hundred canvas curtains blocked out Vietnam's delicate setting sun. I pushed open the large glass doors, walked into the spacious foyer. A pleasant young woman with long black hair sat behind a large wood desk.

"Forty dollar one night," she said.

I thanked her and walked out. It would be dark soon. Where would I eat? Where would I sleep? Undaunted, Nguyen made for Thu Dau Mot's Central Station.

"You go Saigon," he yelled, as the hot wind flattened our hair and pelted our faces. Slowed by evening traffic we entered the depot as the last crowded bus rolled off into the night. "Take taxi!" Nguyen hollered above the urban din.

I hopped off the trembling Cub.

"Here," I said, and flourished money.

"No."

Cars honked, impatient cyclists gunned their engines. We shook hands. Nguyen vanished.

Inside a much-abused American station wagon, twelve skinny passengers vied for impossible comfort. A lovely Chinese woman squished tight against me explained the riddle of Song Be.

"People no understand map. Name change many time in war. Also, some people crazy."

Sweaty and swayed by the sleepless road, we drifted past small, impoverished towns, emerald rice paddies, exhausted peasants hunkering down for the night. Several times I shook myself awake. Weeks, or was it years ago, a Vietnamese monk had warned me, "Always watch your things. The people steal." I dropped my guard and slept.

Waking at Saigon's Long Distance Bus Station I checked my gear, crawled out and headed for the main road. An alert cyclo driver pulled up, and tried to hustle me.

"Where you go? I take. Two dollah. Two dollah. Where you go?"

I shook my head. "Too much," I muttered, shouldered my pack and walked away.

"One dollah."

"No."

"How much? How much?" the desperate voice repeated.

After the brutal re-education camps, where beatings, starvation and slavery were commonplace, many ARVN officers could only find work driving cyclos.

"Fifty cents," I said. The pack grew heavy. Its straps dug into my shoulders.

"OK... OK. Get in." The pedicab groaned forward.

The next morning, after breakfast at the Sinh Café, I flew to Phnom Penh. A stifling cinderblock room with bed and sink at the Capitol Guest House cost three dollars. On the adjacent street I met the cheerful bully called Elephant Man; he had survived Pol Pot and now ferried backpackers on his motorbike. Elephant Man took me to Tuol Sleng, the notorious torture center. We visited the Killing Fields, actually one of thousands across the country. Then I asked Elephant Man to take me to the Ministry of Information.

"Why you want?" he asked.

But I would not tell him. "Just pick me up in two hours," I said.

The clothes of the clerk at the Ministry office hung limp against his body. He knew I was lying. "Here," he said. I filled out a mimeographed form, gave him a one-inch passport photo, presented a counterfeit resume, pressed an American five-dollar bill to his palm.

"You come back one hour." I explored narrow winding side streets, poked my head into shops tucked into stucco buildings weathered delicate shades of pink or blue. I smiled and waved to schoolchildren dressed in white uniforms, their teacher carefully chalking Khmer script on ancient blackboards. I bought Aerograms at a French built post office, then walked back to the Ministry of Information.

"Here," said the clerk, who produced an official gold-stamped and laminated Media Pass. His broad mouth formed a diminutive smile. A survivor's smile. Then he was gone.

Three days later, I used the Pass to spend an extra week at the famous ruins of Angkor Wat. In nearby Siem Reap, I met a burly American who spoke fluent Japanese; a shy Japanese girl on the rebound from a broken love affair. I flew to Sihanoukville, found a backpacker's place, then strolled the tranquil shoreline. One night I met a crazed pot-smoking Boston cab driver named Joe. He introduced me to Alex, a cheerful expatriate Englishman. He was married to a local woman who had escaped death at the hands of the Khmer Rouge, but who acted strangely.

"Why is she like that?" he asked, after describing her symptoms. When I explained the basics of PTSD, all Alex said was, "So *that's* it. So *that's* it." I traveled with a young Frenchman who knew the land and language; took a six-hour taxi to Kampong Cham—found a guide, crossed a river, spent a sweltering day in the hushed serried ranks of a rubber plantation. On the ride back to Phnom Penh, I witnessed firsthand the striking red placards whose skull and bones stood ominous guard over a single word: *MINES!*

I mixed M-150 with *Coke-a-Cola* (liquid extracts of nicotine and caffeine are a potent brew for weary travelers); visited serene monks in secluded monasteries; sat with soft-spoken villagers in airy bamboo shelters; played pool at The Heart of Darkness Bar; shrugged off midnight prostitutes and watered-down drinks.

In short, I had many adventures, though looking back, none as dense with feelings as my travels with Than in Quan Loi. I think of him often and hope he is well.

Marc Levy

20 Whatever You Did in War Will Always be With You

> VA Shrink: *Were you in Vietnam?*
> Vietnam Vet: Yes.
>
> VA Shrink: *When were you there?*
> Vietnam vet: Last night.
>
> —Anonymous

I'm kneeling. Tears streak my face, drip down, fall to earth. It's only my second time in combat. Soon I'll be different. Soon revenge for our dead and wounded will meld with fear, and I will help with the killing and the killing will help me. We're just regular grunts: We make too much noise, we have no special skills, we're not elite. But after a time we get the hang of this war, the rhythm of it. Wait. Engage. Disengage. We call it contact, or movement. We psych ourselves up. "Time to kick ass and take names," we say. And between contact and kicking ass or having our asses kicked there is tension that starts small, then builds and builds until we secretly pray it will happen. That we walk into them or them into us, or we mortar them or they rocket us, then the tension explodes like perfect sex, and afterwards... we're spent. There are days, weeks nothing happens, then terror, instant and deep, then relief, like paradise, since the killing is done and we have buried away the wounded and dead. Until it starts all over again.

That was thirty-seven years ago. Or was it last night? A day, a year, twenty years home from war you may begin to act strange. The shrinks, social workers, group therapists, clinical researchers, each has a different take on what causes PTSD. "It's neurolinguistic." "It's cognitive." "It's biochemical," they chime and chatter. Who cares? Just stop the pain. Just stop it. But where does that pain come from? What's going down? Here is what I know: what you learn in combat you do not easily forget. You drop at the first hint of an ambush falling so fast your helmet still spins in the air. You shoot first and ask questions later. The enemy is an unfeeling slippery bug to be stomped out. You live like an animal. You learn to like killing. Learn to fear and hate the enemy. Hate civilians. Can't trust the bastards. You hate taking prisoners. You'd rather kill them. Why? Because the enemy wants to fuck you up. Kill you, your pals, some new guy doesn't know jack shit, wants to waste your Lieutenant, the whole damn platoon.

After a time you learn what war is: the fish-like iridescent gleam inside a brainless head; the sleek white caterpillar of pulsing human gut; the grotesque tableau of charred bodies frozen stiff; the impossible music made by voices howling beyond human form; pure white bones piercing ruby-ripped flesh; the strange oily feel of blood; the sudden slump of the man next to you. The business of flies on the mouths of the dead.

After a time, to a supernatural degree you learn to live with terror, rage, struck-down sorrow, blocked-out guilt or dumb-struck grief. Yes, the supernatural threat of catastrophe and the ways to survive it become preternaturally normal, second nature, a fully formed part of you.

Then one day you get shot, or if you are lucky, complete the tour, return home intact. But for those who have seen their share the equation might go like this: Johnny got his gun + Johnny marches home = *HEEEREE'S JOHNNNNY!!!!*

And the good soldier John or the good troop Jane, who under fire never once thought of your civil rights, your silly flag, your doofus politics, Good Johnny or Jane, I say, feel and act a tad differently when the locked-down feelings, bottled-up memories, instinctive behaviors of Post Traumatic Stress Disorder fervently, unexpectedly kick in. The symptoms of PTSD, in plain bloody English, are as follows:

- Flashbacks: Seeing and feeling a combat event as if it were happening right now.
- Hypervigilance: Being always on guard, always looking for where the next shot, next grenade, next rocket, ambush or IED will come next.
- Survivor Guilt: Feeling bad, feeling real shitty for having survived, where others in the platoon or squad didn't.
- Moral Guilt: Wrestling with actions one did or did not take on one or more than one occasions.
- Startle Reflex: Dropping, flinching, turning fast at a sudden noise or unexpected touch.
- Suicidal Ideation: Thinking of killing oneself.
- Homicidal Ideation: Thinking of killing people. Friends or complete strangers.

- Homicidal Rage: Anger way out of proportion to an everyday event. It comes quick, down and dirty.
- Sadness, depression, anxiety, crying spells. Staring into space, saying nothing.
- Nightmares: Violent dreams related to combat. Sometimes it's the same dream. Some vets make strange noises. Thrash in bed. Wake up scared, or sweaty.
- Ritual Behavior: At night checking the lights, locking the doors, maybe keeping a weapon at hand.
- Alienation: A vet feels as if no one understands him, doesn't fit in, feels as if he or she should have never returned.
- Panic Attacks: For a short time the combat vet becomes suddenly and intensely afraid. He or she sweats, breathes hard, has a pounding heart, might get dizzy, choke.
- Social Isolation: Staying alone for long periods of time. Or in public saying very little. To the point of being noticeably very quiet.
- Drug and Alcohol Abuse: Whatever works to dull the pain glowing inside one's head.
- Fear of Emotional Intimacy: Combat vets often won't let anyone get close to them. If someone gets too close, the vet backs off or pushes them away.
- Employment: A lot of vets can't keep a job. Every couple of months quit or get fired.
- Psychic Numbing: Not have the ability to feel emotions. Vets talk about feeling hollow, blank, empty.
- Denial: Problems? *What problem? I don't have a fuckin' problem.*
- High Risk Behaviors: Doing daredevil stuff to re-live the rush of combat.

These symptoms are normal responses to extraordinary events outside the range of normal human experience. Most civilians are clueless about combat and its aftermath.

Some types of treatment

The talking cure: a vet talks to a therapist who is skilled in treating war stress and is not a paid bullshitter.

Group therapy: seven to ten vets meet once a week for an hour or two. A good group leader is essential. That person knows when to talk, when to listen, how to keep the vets focused. Otherwise group therapy can get lame fast.

EMDR: a form of hypnosis in which the vet is fully awake.

Exercise. Meditation. Meds. A friend who will just listen. An artistic endeavor.

One other thing. This is real important: a lot of vets fear talking about war. They fear losing control. Breaking down. Crying. My advice to those who have seen combat: face yourself. Chances are good you will learn to live less in the past, more in the present, but you will never be the same. WWII, Korea, Panama, Viet Nam, Iraq, Afghanistan, Central America, wherever you were, whatever you did in war will always be with you. Always.

About The Contributors

David Bianchini did two tours in Viet Nam as a point man on a LRRP team. He worked in the music business for eight years and married Laura Nyro. He served ten years in prison for growing pot. Presently, he paint, sculpts, and runs a construction company to make money so he can eat lobster tails and drink decent vodka.

Richard Boes is a Viet Nam veteran who suffers from Post Traumatic Stress Disorder. *The Last Dead Soldier Left Alive* is his personal experiential account—a firsthand inquiry into why thousands of Viet Nam veterans have committed suicide. He has a BA in Literature and a Masters in Film. He lives alone in upstate New York, in an apartment he deems a glorified bunker.

Don Bodey was drafted into the Army in 1969. His semi-autobiographical account of survival in Viet Nam was eventually published as the award-winning *F.N.G.* in 1985. Bodey went on to teach creative writing at the college level and is active in encouraging veterans to get their feelings down on paper. He currently lives near Ft. Wayne, Indiana with his wife Annie. A newly revised edition of *F.N.G.* is available from Modern History Press.

Alan Farrell is a longtime professor who taught French and English at Hampden-Sydney College for nearly twenty-five years before coming to VMI. He holds a BA—Cum Laude and Phi Beta Kappa—from Trinity College in Hartford, CT, a Master's in German and a Doctorate in French from Tufts University in Boston. He served in Viet Nam with the famous Fifth Special Forces Group, was wounded in action, decorated for heroism. He was designated by the Governor as Distinguished Foreign Language Professor in Virginia and earned the Virginia Association of Foreign Language Teachers' Distinguished Service Award. Dean of Faculty from 1996 until 2000, he teaches French at VMI

Preston Hood's poems have appeared in *Animus, The Café Review, Cyphers, Icarus, Main Street Rag, Michigan Quarterly Review, Nimrod: International Journal, Poetry Motel, Rattle, Salamander* and many other literary publications. His poem, "Boats Near Hue, Viet Nam, 1997" won Honorable Mention in *Writer's Digest* 73rd non-rhyming poetry category. In 2002, he produced a poetry CD, *Snake Medicine.* In 2005, he was awarded a residency at Heinrich Boll Cottage on Achill Island in County Mayo, Ireland where he completed his manuscript, *A Chill I Understand.* This book won Honorable Mention in the 2007 Maine Literary Awards for published poetry.

Marc Levy served with Delta 1/7 Cav as an infantry medic in Viet Nam and Cambodia in 1970. He was decorated once for gallantry, twice for valor, and twice court-martialed. His prose, poetry and essays have been published in various online and print journals, most recently on counterpunch.org. In 2001 he was selected to attend an ACA residence. A video of his war experiences, *The Real Deal*, is distributed by The Cinema Guild. He is profiled in *Inconvenient Stories: Viet Nam War Veterans*, by Jeff Wolin.

David W. Powell was a computer programmer who enlisted in the Marines after receiving a draft notice in 1966. He served as a rocketman (MOS 0351) on Hill 55 and Hill 41 in Chu Lai and Da Nang. After suffering for two decades with what would eventually be christened PTSD, he has since returned to normal life. He credits his recovery to a technique called Traumatic Incident Reduction (TIR). His memoir *My Tour In Hell: A Marine's Battle with Combat Trauma* was published in 2006. He currently lives in Tucson, Arizona with his wife Susan.

Tom Skiens was born in Burns Oregon June 21, 1947. Graduated from high school in 1966. He joined the 11th light infantry brigade in Hawaii, September 1967. Tom became the 4.2 inch Forward Observer (FO) for Charlie Company, 4th Battalion 3d Infantry Regiment on the USS General Gordon seven days before we arrived in Viet Nam. He later attended Southern Oregon State College from 1969 through 1974. He has conducted critical incident debriefings, conducted 4 interventions, given classes and trained about substance abuse and critical incident stress.

Tony Swindell served with the 31st PID, 11th Light Infantry Brigade, Americal Division, during 1968-69. His unit participated in the My Lai massacre in Pinkville in 1968, and he was later a witness to incidents involving the murder of Vietnamese civilians by brigade commander Col. John W. Donaldson. He is currently an editor at the Sherman, Texas, *Herald Democrat*.

Victor R. Volkman is the Senior Editor of Modern History Press. Although not a veteran, he is committed that veterans' stories be told. He edited *My Tour In Hell: A Marine's Battle with Combat Trauma*, consulted with Rick Ritter on *Made In America, 2nd Ed.*, and edited *Giving My Heart: Love in a Military Family* by Lisa Farber-Silk. In 2007, he helped organize the Vermont Veterans Combat Stress Symposium.

Dayl S. Wise was drafted into the US Army in 1969 and served in Vietnam and Cambodia in 1970 with the First Air Cav. He lives part time in the Bronx and Woodstock, New York with his wife, Alison Koffler, a poet; Molly, a Labrador-pit bull mix and Six, a calico cat with a bad leg. He is the editor of *Post Traumatic Press 2008*, a collection of poems by veterans.

Glossary

[Ed Note: although originally begun for the purpose of describing Viet Nam slang, it quickly became apparent that a wider audience could be reached by including all military terms used throughout the entire work.]

4-F: Classification given to those deemed unfit for military service (see also Draft Board).

82: 82 mm mortar used by the Viet Cong.

A-Gunner: an Assistant Gunner is needed for many heavier weapons to make them practical in the field. The duties vary depending on the weapon.

Agent Orange: Agent Orange is the code name for a powerful herbicide and defoliant used by the US military in its Herbicidal Warfare program during the Viet Nam War. Agent Orange was used from 1961 to 1971, and was by far the most used of the so-called "rainbow herbicides" used during the program. Containing dioxins, now known to be notorious carcinogen, it attacked both friend and foe alike.

AK-47: Soviet-manufactured Kalashnikov semi-automatic and fully automatic combat assault rifle, 7.62 mm; the basic weapon of the Communist forces. Known as the 'Type 56' to the Chinese, it is characterized by an explosive popping sound.

Arty: Short for "Artillery".

Arc Light: Code name for B-52 bomber strikes along the Cambodian-Vietnamese border. These operations shook the earth for ten miles away from the target area.

Article 15: Section of the Uniform Code of Military Justice (UCMJ). A form of non-judicial punishment for minor offenses. The accused might or might not be granted a hearing if requested.

ARVN: Army of the Republic of (South) Viet Nam.

B-40: A shoulder-held rocket-propelled grenade launcher used by the NVA. A variant of the Russian RPG-2, ancestor of the RPG-7.

Bad paper: More than 560,000 less-than-honorable discharges were issued in the Viet Nam era. Bad-paper holders are not eligible for veterans' benefits until the document is upgraded to an honorable or a general discharge.

Basic (Basic Training): The initial period of training for new military personnel; involves intense physical activity and behavioral discipline. Around nine weeks, depending on service branch and era.

Battalion S-2: The Battalion is the smallest Army unit which has a Headquarters Staff. There are four Staff offices, numbered S1 through S4. The S2 is responsible for Intelligence. It gathers local intelligence, interprets and analyzes it, maintains files of intelligence sent to the Battalion by higher HQ, and sends the Intelligence it gathers back up the chain of command.

Bird Dog: O-1 aircraft were used by Forward Air Controllers (FACS) for reconnaissance. A "FAC", often an experienced fighter pilot, was assigned to a specific geographical area, so that he could readily identify enemy activity. If a FAC observed enemy ground targets, he marked them with smoke rockets so they could be easily attacked by fighter-bombers. The FAC remained near the scene to report bombing results.

Blouse: Marines refer to any shirt as a blouse.

Boat People: Events resulting from the Viet Nam War led many people in Cambodia, Laos, and especially Viet Nam to become refugees in the late 1970s and 1980s, after the fall of Saigon. In Viet Nam, the new communist government sent many people who supported the old government in the South to "re-education camps", and others to "new economic zones." These factors, coupled with poverty caused by disastrous economic reforms, caused millions of Vietnamese to flee the country. On the open seas, the boat people had to confront forces of nature, and elude pirates.

Boot (Camp): See Basic.

Bouncing Betty: Antipersonnel explosive that propels upward about four feet into the air and then detonates.

Buckle for Dust: To fight, as in combat.

C-rat (C-ration): Literally "Combat Rations". Canned meals for use in the field. Each ration consisted of a canned entree, a "B-2 unit" containing cheese, crackers and candy, a canned dessert, and an accessory pack. The accessory pack contained a P-38 can opener, mix for a hot beverage, salt and sugar packets, plastic spoon, chewing gum, a pack of four cigarettes and several sheets of toilet paper.

Cam On Ong: "Thank you" (Vietnamese).

CAR-15: CAR-15 has a meaning split between closely related firearms, which depends on the context. In popular usage it is a general name applied to many ultra-short and carbine variants of the Colt AR-15 rifle (adopted by the USA as the M-16 rifle).

CB: Combat Base.

Glossary

Charlie: American forces typically referred to members of the National Liberation Front as "Charlie," which comes from the US Armed Forces' phonetic alphabet's pronunciation of VC ("Victor Charlie"). See *Viet Cong*.

Chieu Hoi: Translation "Open Arms". A program to actively take in defectors from the NVA. Also refers to a person who is a defector.

CIB: (Combat Infantry Badge) The Army award for serving as an Infantryman in a combat zone for 30 days or more, or for being wounded while serving as an Infantryman in combat.

Claymore (M-18): A directional antipersonnel fragmentation mine containing 700 steel spheres and 1.5 pounds of C-4 explosives detonated by an electrically activated blasting cap. It has a kill zone of 50 meters in a 60-degree swath to the front. Backblast is dangerous to 100 meters in the rear from secondary effects.

CO: Commanding Officer.

Cobra: Bell AH-1 "Cobra" was a combat workhorse in the later years of the Viet Nam War beginning with the TET Offensive of 1968. It carried a crew of two armed with 20 mm cannons, TOW missiles, and 70 mm rockets.

Conex: Corrugated metal packing crate, approximately six feet in length.

CP (Check Point): A landmark used as a reference on road patrols. Usually a bridge that required a manned watch at night. CPs were manned by a squad of ARVN who lived there and assisted by an MP patrol.

CQ: (charge of quarters) An officer officially in charge of a unit headquarters at night.

CS: A nonlethal riot-control gas which burns the eyes and mucus membranes. Commonly used to flush Viet Cong from tunnels.

Currahee: A Cherokee word meaning literally "stands alone". The word was adopted by WWII paratrooper units including the legendary 101st Airborne and aptly describes their role in combat.

DI: Drill Instructor.

didi or "di di": (sometimes written as "dee dee") Slang from the Vietnamese word *di*, meaning "to leave" or "to go".

DMZ (Demilitarized Zone): In military terms, a demilitarized zone (DMZ) is an area, usually the frontier or boundary between two or more groups, where military activity is not permitted, usually by treaty or other agreement. Often the demilitarized zone lies upon a line of control and forms a de facto international border.

Dinks: Racial epithet for Vietnamese. Reputedly short for "rinky dink" (worthless) or perhaps from the Vietnamese phrase "dinky dau" meaning "crazy". Same usage as gooks or slopes.

Draft Board: A Selective Service Local Board is a group of five citizen volunteers whose mission, upon a draft, will be to decide who among the registrants in their community will receive deferments, postponements, or exemption from military service based on the individual registrant's circumstances and beliefs. Members of a Draft Board are never military or law enforcement officers.

Dusted Off: Evacuated by helicopter. The helicopter raises a lot of dust on landing and take-off, therefore dusted off means airlifted.

E-6: Rank of Staff Sergeant (*see*) in the US Army or Marines.

Eltee: Vocalization of "LT" or "Lt.", as in the abbreviation for Lieutenant.

Field of Fire: The area around a weapon (or group of weapons) which can be easily and effectively reached by gun fire. Fields of fire today are mostly used in reference to machine guns.

Firebase (FSB): A Fire Support Base (FSB) is an encampment designed to provide fire support to infantry operating in areas beyond the normal range of their main base camp cannon and howitzers. FSBs were used extensively in the Viet Nam War.

FLA: (Front-Line Ambulance) M718 Jeep with slightly extended cargo area for stretchers.

Flak Jacket: During the Viet Nam War, many soldiers, Marines and Airmen received vests that would stop shrapnel, but not a bullet. In the Viet Nam climate they were hot and uncomfortable, and felt heavy and bulky. Nonetheless, they were widely adopted and the soldier in his flak vest became a symbol of the war.

Flame Tank: M-67 "Zippo". Although much safer than man-carried flamethrowers, the flame tanks suffered vulnerability to anti-tank weapons on the battlefield due to the relatively short range of fire-based weaponry.

FO: Forward Observer.

Frags: Fragmentation grenades.

FNG (Fucking New Guy): The New Guy was the most dangerous person to have around because he would not know the hazards and might get you killed or maimed.

Freedom Bird: The flight that would take you back to the US after your tour in Viet Nam was done.

FTA: Fuck The Army. Perhaps a play on the Army's recruiting mantra of "Fun, Travel, and Adventure."

Get Some: Common expression meaning "to kill the enemy."

Gooks: Racial epithet for Vietnamese.

Grease: to kill. c.f. "grease gun"

Grunt: The term grunt is slang for an infantryman in the US Army and Marines. Infantrymen are known to take extreme pride in the term. It was used especially in the Viet Nam War.

GSW: Gun Shot Wound.

Guard Mounting: A.k.a. the Changing of the Guard, refers to a formal ceremony in which sentries providing ceremonial guard duties at important institutions are relieved by a new batch of sentries.

Gun Truck: Standard cargo truck with added armor and machineguns for convoy escort.

Hearts and Minds: Hearts and Minds was a euphemism for a campaign by the United States military during the Viet Nam War, intended to win the popular support of the Vietnamese people. There is little evidence to show that it was anything other than pro-war propaganda, and rang hollow compared to anti-war publicity efforts. The eponymous film (1974) showed the inherent contradictions of the term, and the term "Hearts and Minds" remains symbolic of the fictional nature of militarist propaganda.

Highway 1: This was the route from the north into Saigon. Generals Seamans & De Puy with the Big Red One from Dian went up this route to clear it in 1966 so that the rice harvest could get into the city

Ho Chi Minh Trail: named after Ho Chi Minh, leader of the revolution. It was a vast NVA and VC supply route

Hooch: Building made of bamboo and covered with a thatched roof. Built on stilts to protect it from flooding.

Huey: refers to Bell Huey Cobra helicopter (see entry "Cobra")

I Corps: The northernmost military region in South Viet Nam.

Joe (G.I. Joe): The archetypal foot soldier. Coined by Dave Breger in the eponymous comic strip on June 17th, 1942.

Jungle Rot: Jungle rot is equivalent to athlete's foot and is caused by a combination of heat and moisture due to Viet Nam's tropical climate.

KA-BAR: Combat knife with a six-inch blade and hard leather handle, used mostly by the Marine Corps.

KIA: Killed in Action.

Kill Zone: Area in front of an ambush that the maximum fire power is directed at. Alternately, the radius of a circle around an explosive device within which it is predicted that 95 percent of all occupants will be killed should the device explode

KP: Kitchen Patrol, e.g. washing dishes, peeling potatoes, etc.

LAW: Light Anti-Tank Weapon (LAW), see M72

Lifer: Career military man. The term is often used in a derogatory manner.

LOCH: Light Observation / Cargo Helicopter. Typically the OH-6 Cayuse (nickname **"Loach"**). This two-seater was easily recognizable by its egg-shaped glass canopy and could carry six people.

LP: Listening post. A two- or three-man position set up at night outside the perimeter away from the main body of troopers, which acted as an early warning system against attack.

LRRP: (Long-Range Reconnaissance Patrol) Pronounced "lurp." An elite team usually composed of five to seven men who go deep into the jungle to observe enemy activity without initiating contact.

LZ: Landing Zone, point at where infantry are inserted or extracted from the countryside.

M-14: First deployed in 1962, the M-14 was unwieldy in the thick brush due to its length and weight. The power of the 7.62 mm NATO cartridge allowed it to penetrate cover quite well and reach out to extended range. The M-14 remained the primary infantry weapon in Viet Nam until replacement by the M-16 in 1966—1968

M-60: The M-60 Machine Gun was introduced in 1957 by the US Army. It fires the standard NATO 7.62 mm round and is used as a general support crew-served weapon. It has a removable barrel which can be easily changed to prevent overheating. The weapon has an integral, folding bipod and can also be mounted on a folding tripod.

M-79: Hand-held grenade launcher.

MACV: Military Assistance Command, Viet Nam.

Medevac (Medivac): Medical Evacuation of wounded, normally by helicopter unless otherwise specified.

Glossary

MIA: Missing In Action. A soldier who has disappeared during combat action, status unknown.

Minigun: When the US entered the Viet Nam War during early 1960s, it found it needed to arm its helicopters to provide additional firepower against enemy infantry. The Minigun, essentially an M-60 machine gun with six barrels, could fire up to 4,000 rounds per minute and was soon adapted to the various helicopter mounts (including the AH-1 Cobra and UH1 "Huey").

Montagnards: (a.k.a. Mountain-Yards or just 'Yards) Literally French for 'mountain dweller'. In Viet Nam they were often persecuted by the Communists. Easily identified because they are short in stature and darker than the lowland Vietnamese. In many ways, they could be compared to the Native American.

MPC: Military Payment Certificates, were used from the end of World War II until the end of the Viet Nam War. MPCs utilized layers of line lithography to create colorful banknotes that could be produced cheaply. They were issued to servicemen in the field to prevent local economies from being flooded with US dollars.

NCO: (Non-Commissioned Officer) The NCO is often referred to as "the backbone" of the military services. NCOs and POs are the primary and most visible leaders for the bulk of Service personnel – the enlisted corps. Additionally, NCOs are the primary military leaders responsible for executing the military organization's mission—and for training the personnel in an organization so they are prepared to execute the mission.

OCS: Officer Candidate School.

ODs: "Olive Drabs", the standard Army green color of uniforms.

ONI: Office of Naval Intelligence. In the Viet Nam era, ONI would investigate alleged mutinies, drug use among Marines and other crimes.

Operation Phoenix: A CIA-run covert program designed to capture, kill, or otherwise neutralize the Viet Cong Infrastructure (VCI) cadres who were engaged both in recruiting and training insurgents within South Vietnamese villages as well as providing support to the North Vietnamese war effort.

Orange Mist: See Agent Orange

Pathet Lao: Laotian equivalent of the Viet Minh and the Viet Cong of Viet Nam.

PFC: Private First Class. In the US Army, PFC is the third lowest enlisted rank, just above Private and below Corporal or Specialist. Often earned after six months as a Private.

POW: Prisoner of War.

Primer cord: A thin, flexible tube with an explosive core. It is a high-speed fuse which explodes, rather than burns, and is suitable for detonating high explosives. c.f. "Primacord", a brand name for this product.

PSGT: Platoon Sergeant. Highest ranking NCO in a platoon (about two dozen men).

Punji Stakes: Punji stakes were bamboo stalks, about a foot long, sharpened to a point on one end. The VC stuck them in the ground, pointed end up, hoping we would step, or fall, on them. The tip of the punji stick was frequently smeared with feces, urine, poison, or other contaminants to promote infection in the wound created by the sharpened stick penetrating the soldier's skin.

QTCB: Quang Tri Combat Base.

Repl-Depl: Literally, 'Replacement-Deployment'. An infantry outfit where additional training is provided just prior to deployment.

Rock Pile: The Rock Pile is the rocky hill used to be the American firepower base in 1966. Rock Pile had no way to go up or down, therefore troops only received resupply by helicopter.

RPG (Rocket Propelled Grenade): The RPG-7 anti-tank weapon was first deployed by the Soviets in 1961. Similar in use and function as the M-20 used by American forces. Still in use by Iraqi insurgents today.

RTO: Radio/Telephone Operator (RTO). One half of the Forward Observer team.

Ruck: Rucksack (backpack) had to carry everything for a soldier in the field. Usually with a metal frame for stability and support.

Rung Sat: A jungle where the North Vietnamese Army (NVA) and Viet Cong (VC) infiltrated South Vietnam.

Screaming Eagles: Nickname of the 101st Airborne.

Seabees: The Naval Mobile Construction Battalion is known by the phonetic pronunciation of their initials (CBs = "see-bees").

Shake and Bake: Sergeant who attended NCO school and earned rank after only a very short time in uniform.

Sitrep: (Situation Report) a regular communications check between units in the field and the rear

Glossary

Sixteen: Refers to M-16 assault rifle, introduced into Viet Nam in 1967.

Sixty: Refers to M-60 machine gun. It provides a higher rate of fire, greater effective range, and uses a larger caliber round than the standard-issue US assault rifle, the M-16. Weight 23 pounds, unloaded.

Staff Sergeant (SSG or SSgt): The staff sergeant is a more experienced leader of soldiers and will often have one or more sergeants under his direct leadership. SSGs are the elements from which the backbones of the US Army and Marines are made.

Steel Pot: Helmet.

TET Offensive: An operation which began on lunar New Year's night, January 30th, 1968. Although a sound military defeat for the Communist forces, it nevertheless was an enormous propaganda victory for the NLF and PAVN.

Tetrytol: Tetrytol is a cast mixture of tetryl and TNT and is designed to obtain a tetryl mixture that may be used in burster tubes for chemical bombs, in demolition blocks, and in cast shaped-charges.

VA (Veteran's Administration): US Department of Veterans Affairs. Of the 25 million veterans currently alive in 2006, nearly three of every four served during a war or an official period of hostility.

Viet Cong ("VC"): From the Vietnamese term for Vietnamese Communist (Việt Nam Cộng Sản).

Ville: French word literally meaning "village". May refer to any indigenous encampment in Viet Nam.

ZILs: Russian all-purpose trucks used in Vietnam

Index

1

101st Airborne, 211, 216

A

Afghanistan, 204
Agent Orange, 24, 25, 52, 58, 192, 209, 215
A-Gunner, 32
AK-47, 209
American Servicemen's Union, 109–19
An Loc, 191, 193, 194, 195
Angkor Wat, 160
Aponte, W., 109–19
Arc Light, 70, 71, 125–31, 180, 209
ARVN, 145, 209, 211

B

Berry, B.H., 116
Bianchini, D., 181
Binh Long, 191, 193, 195
Bird Dog, 170, 210
Bodey, D., 51–63
Bouncing Betty, 74, 187, 210

C

Cam Ranh Bay, 22, 178
Cambodia, 101, 157, 158, 163, 194, 206, 207, 209, 210
Camp Pendleton, 111, 115
Camp Zama, 26
Chieu Hoi, 101, 180, 211
Christmas, 140, 144, 178
Chu Lai, 73, 133, 135, 145, 206
Claymore, 14, 71, 84, 107, 164, 211
Cobra (AH-1), 215
CS gas, 187
Currahee, 211

D

Da Nang, 26, 166, 169, 206
Daniels, G., 109–19
depression, 203
Detroit, 111
Dishonorable Discharge, 101
DMZ, 178, 211

F

Fant, L.G., 115
Farrell, A., 21–23, 43, 88–91, 123, 125, 149
FNG, 15, 143
Fort Belvoir, 177
Fort Benning, 177
Fort Carson, 158
Fort Hood, 109, 118
Forward Observer, 212, 216
Freedom Bird, 213
Ft. Devens, 100

G

Galloway, J., 83
Gerbode, F.A., 172

H

Harvey, W., 109–19
heroin, 172, 173, 174
Highway 13, 196
Hilgers, J., 112
Hill 170, iii
Hill 54, 133
Hill 55, 31, 36, 41, 172, 206
Hill 881, 26
Ho Chi Minh Trail, 125, 131, 213
Hood, P., 24, 44, 67, 79, 147
Huey, 215
hypervigilance, 173, 202

J

Jenkins, 31, 32
Jolls, S., 109–19

K

KA-BAR, 77, 127, 182, 214
Khe Sanh, 26
Khmer Rouge, 161, 163, 199
Korea, 153

L

LAAW, 37
LaGrande, Oregon, 76
Laos, 210

Levine, R., 48, 65, 68, 80, 92
Levy, M., 49, 70, 93–108, 148
Loc Ninh, 195
LOCH, 214
LZ Bronco, 30, 87, 133
LZ Buzzard, 28
LZ Carentan, 138, 139
LZ Compton, 192, 195, 196
LZ Lucy, 81
LZ Sue, 133, 136, 138, 143

M

M-188, 149
M-60, 76, 188
M-79, 97
Marble Mountain, 169
mast, 111
Memorial Day, 47, 95
MPC, 215
Murphy, J., 83

N

New Guy, 34
nickname, 214, 216
nightmares, 32, 41, 86, 203
North Vietnamese, 215
NVA, 209, 211

O

ONI, 112, 115, 116, 167
Operation Foster, 169, 170
Operation Phoenix, 215

P

Parris Island, 166
Pentagon, 110, 114, 115, 118
Phnom Penh, 158, 164, 198, 199
point man, 101, 167, 168, 205
Pol Pot, 198
Portsmouth, N.H., 109
Powell, D.W., 31–41
Preah Khan, 157
protest, 41
PTSD, 165, 173, 199, 202
punji stakes, 34, 181, 216
Purple Heart, 31, 37, 38, 39, 97, 101, 104, 105, 106, 176

Q

QTCB, 216
Quan Loi, 102, 191, 193, 199
Quang Ngai, 30
Quang Tri, 26, 83, 216
Qui Nhon, 22, 133, 139
Quonset hut, 44

R

Raitano, R., 133–45
Ray, M.H., 27
Read, H., 23
Red Cross, 133
Repl-Depl, 216
Rock Pile, 216
Rung Sat, 24
Russia, 209

S

S-2, 133, 210
Saigon, 27, 31, 111, 178, 210
Sassoon, S., v, 46
Schofield Barracks, 134
Shapiro, K., 21
Siem Reap, 160, 199
Skiens, T., 187
sleep disturbances, 41, *See also* Nightmares
Song Be, 50, 196, 198
Song Tra Khuc, 73
South China Sea, 73, 79
startle reaction, 32, 40
survivor guilt, 202
Swindell, T., 46, 86

T

Ta'Prom, 162
TAOR, 167
TET Offensive, 145, 211, 217
Thach Han River, 84
Thailand, 8
Tokyo, 41
Trautwein, H.J., 114
Tunnele Sap River, 158, 164

U

USS Gordon, 133, 137

V

VA hospital, 172
Viet Cong, 31, 33, 36, 209, 211, 215, 217
Viet Nam Veterans Memorial, 65–66
vomit, 37

W

Warnecki, 31
West Point, 176
Wise, D., 28, 45, 69, 72, 81, 121, 155
World War II, 153, 211, 215

Z

Zippo, 73

www.ingramcontent.com/pod-product-compliance
Lightning Source LLC
Chambersburg PA
CBHW081916170426
43200CB00014B/2747